P9-BYR-813

WHILE THE WORLD WATCHED

WHILE THE WORLD WATCHED

A Birmingham Bombing Survivor
Comes of Age during the Civil Rights Movement

Carolyn Maull McKinstry
with Denise George

Visit Tyndale online at www.tyndale.com.

TYNDALE and Tyndale's quill logo are registered trademarks of Tyndale House Publishers, Inc.

While the World Watched: A Birmingham Bombing Survivor Comes of Age during the Civil Rights Movement

Copyright © 2011 by Carolyn McKinstry. All rights reserved.

Cover photograph of author and interior photograph of author in church by Stephen Vosloo copyright © Tyndale House Publishers, Inc. All rights reserved.

Cover and interior photograph of Birmingham street used with the permission of the Birmingham, Alabama, Public Library Archives, Cat. #85.1.9.

Cover and interior photographs of four girls; caskets; mourners on street; grieving mother; civil rights leaders; Justice Department demonstration; policemen outside church; and Dr. Martin Luther King Jr. copyright © AP Images. All rights reserved.

Photograph of demonstrators being hosed copyright © Charles Moore/Black Star. All rights reserved.

Photograph of police dogs attacking young man copyright © Bill Hudson/AP Images. All rights reserved.

All other photographs are from the personal collection of the author and used with permission.

Background texture pattern copyright © Morgan Lane Photography/Shutterstock. All rights reserved.

The following speech excerpts are reprinted by arrangement with The Heirs to the Estate of Martin Luther King Jr., c/o Writers House as agent for the proprietor New York, NY:

"Letter from a Birmingham Jail," copyright © 1963 Dr. Martin Luther King Jr.; copyright renewed 1991 Coretta Scott King.

"Where Do We Go from Here?" copyright © 1967 Dr. Martin Luther King Jr.; copyright renewed 1995 Coretta Scott King.

"I Have a Dream," copyright © 1963 Dr. Martin Luther King Jr.; copyright renewed 1991 Coretta Scott King.

"I've Been to the Mountaintop," copyright © 1968 Dr. Martin Luther King Jr.; copyright renewed 1996 Coretta Scott King.

"Nobel Prize Acceptance Speech," copyright © 1964 Dr. Martin Luther King Jr.; copyright renewed 1992 Coretta Scott King.

Funeral speech for the slain girls, copyright © 1963 Dr. Martin Luther King Jr.; copyright renewed 1991 Coretta Scott King.

Designed by Jessie McGrath

Edited by Stephanie Rische

Published in association with the literary agency of WordServe Literary Group, Ltd., 10152 S. Knoll Circle, Highlands Ranch, CO 80130.

All Scripture quotations, unless otherwise indicated, are taken from the Holy Bible, *New International Version,*® *NIV.*® Copyright © 1973, 1978, 1984 by Biblica, Inc.™ Used by permission of Zondervan. All rights reserved worldwide. www.zondervan.com.

Scripture quotations marked KJV are taken from the *Holy Bible*, King James Version.

Scripture quotations marked NKJV are taken from the New King James Version.® Copyright © 1982 by Thomas Nelson, Inc. Used by permission. All rights reserved.

Library of Congress Cataloging-in-Publication Data

McKinstry, Carolyn Maull, date.
 While the world watched : a Birmingham bombing survivor comes of age during the civil rights movement / Carolyn Maull McKinstry with Denise George.
  p. cm.
 Includes bibliographical references.
 ISBN 978-1-4143-3636-7 (hc)
  1. McKinstry, Carolyn Maull, date. 2. 16th Street Baptist Church Bombing, Birmingham, Ala., 1963. 3. Civil rights movements—Alabama—Birmingham—History—20th century. 4. African Americans—Alabama—Birmingham—Biography. 5. Birmingham (Ala.)—Social conditions. 6. Birmingham (Ala.)—Biography. I. George, Denise. II. Title.
 F334.B653M356 2011
 976.1'781063—dc22   2010047575

ISBN 978-1-4143-3637-4 (sc)

Printed in the United States of America

18 17 16 15 14
 6   5   4   3

This book is dedicated to my grandparents,
Reverend Ernest Walter and Lessie V. Burt,
whose prayers sustained us and whose wisdom and love
still live within me and my family;

my parents, Samuel and Ernestine Burt Maull,
who gave us their absolute best and prepared us in such
a loving way for the rough road that lay ahead;

my husband, Jerome McKinstry, whom God sent
in the midst of all my pain and confusion and who
still stands today as a cornerstone for me; and

my children—Leigh, Joya, and Brandon—
who are the fruit and the joys of my life and who
have made this struggle worth every day.

Finally and especially, this book is dedicated
to the memory of my friends Addie Mae Collins,
Carol Denise McNair, Carole Robertson, and
Cynthia Wesley, killed September 15, 1963,
when Sixteenth Street Baptist Church was bombed,
and to the memory of Johnny Robinson and Virgil
Ware, also killed September 15, 1963, who now laugh
and walk with Addie, Denise, Carole, and Cynthia.

May they all rest in peace and in the knowledge
that their story and their witness live on in the
hearts of people of goodwill all over the world.

—C. M. M.

Contents

Introduction

Almost half a century has passed since the Klan bombed Sixteenth Street Baptist Church at 10:22 on Sunday morning, September 15, 1963, and my four young friends died agonizing deaths. And it's been almost half a century since, as a young teen, I marched under the leadership of Dr. Martin Luther King Jr. and got a handful of hair torn from my scalp by Bull Connor's powerful water hoses.

For twenty years after these experiences, I tried hard to forget the senseless deaths, the inhumane injustices, the vicious German shepherds, and children getting arrested right on the streets of downtown Birmingham. In fact, we were encouraged by our parents, other church members, and our black community to forget what had happened. For almost five decades, I had not been able to muster the courage, nor the composure, to publicly record the stories that have become such a dark part of our nation's past. I had struggled to forget these stories, to rid them from my head and heart. They proved too horrible, too painful, to dredge up to memory.

But now, as I see new generations coming and old generations passing, I feel compelled to remember, to write down in permanent ink my eyewitness account of just what happened while the world watched . . . lest *I* forget. Lest *we all* forget.

I hope this story will challenge you to reexamine your life; your daily living; your values; and your relationship with God, our Creator. As you consider the events on these pages, may you choose to love, and may you commit yourself to live a life of reconciliation—first with God and then ultimately with those who share this world with you.

Carolyn Maull McKinstry
SPRING 2011

THE CIVIL RIGHTS MOVEMENT ...
THROUGH THE EYES OF
CAROLYN MAULL McKINSTRY

1948

JANUARY 13, 1948:
Carolyn Maull is born in Clanton, Alabama.

1954

MAY 17, 1954:
Supreme Court bans segregation in schools in the
Brown v. Board of Education *decision.*

1955

AUGUST 28, 1955:
*Fourteen-year-old Emmett Till is kidnapped and
murdered in Mississippi.*

DECEMBER 1, 1955:
*Rosa Parks is arrested for refusing to give up her seat
to a white in Montgomery, Alabama.*

DECEMBER 5, 1955:
Montgomery bus boycott begins.

1956

NOVEMBER 13, 1956:
Supreme Court affirms ban on segregated seating on Alabama buses.

DECEMBER 25, 1956:
Reverend Fred Shuttlesworth's house in Birmingham is bombed.

1957

SEPTEMBER 2, 1957:
Klan members kidnap and castrate Edward Aaron in Birmingham.

SEPTEMBER 24, 1957:
The "Little Rock Nine" enter Central High under the protection of the United States Army's 101st Airborne Division.

1961

1961:
Freedom Rides begin from Washington, D.C., into Southern states.

JANUARY 20, 1961:
John F. Kennedy is inaugurated as president of the United States.

1962

FEBRUARY 26, 1962:
The Supreme Court rules that segregation is unconstitutional in all transportation facilities.

1963

JANUARY 14, 1963:
Newly elected Alabama governor George C. Wallace takes the oath of office.

APRIL 12, 1963:
Dr. King is arrested and locked up in a Birmingham jail.

MAY 2–3, 1963:
Children's marches in downtown Birmingham are broken up by police with attack dogs and fire hoses.

JUNE 11, 1963:
Alabama governor George Wallace stands in the doorway of University of Alabama to try to keep Vivian Malone and James Hood from enrolling.

JUNE 12, 1963:
Klan member kills Mississippi Civil Rights leader Medgar Evers.

AUGUST 28, 1963:
Dr. Martin Luther King Jr. leads march on Washington, D.C., with more than 250,000 people in attendance.

SEPTEMBER 15, 1963:
A bomb planted at Sixteenth Street Baptist Church explodes and kills four girls.

SEPTEMBER 15, 1963:
Virgil Ware, 13, is killed in Birmingham by two white youth; Johnny Robinson, 16, is killed by police in Birmingham.

SEPTEMBER 30, 1963:
Police arrest Robert Chambliss, Charles Cagle, and John W. Hall in conjunction with the Sixteenth Street Church bombing; they are released after each paying a $100 fine.

NOVEMBER 22, 1963:
President John F. Kennedy is assassinated in Dallas, Texas.

1964

JULY 2, 1964:
President Lyndon B. Johnson signs the Civil Rights Act of 1964.

OCTOBER 14, 1964:
Dr. Martin Luther King Jr. is awarded the Nobel Peace Prize for advocating a policy of nonviolence.

1965

FEBRUARY 21, 1965:
Malcolm X is assassinated.

MARCH 25, 1965:
Martin Luther King Jr. leads thousands of nonviolent crusaders to the completion of a 54-mile pilgrimage from Selma to Montgomery.

AUGUST 6, 1965:
President Johnson signs the Voting Rights Act outlawing literacy tests for voting eligibility in the South.

1967

OCTOBER 2, 1967:
Thurgood Marshall is sworn in as the first black Supreme Court justice.

1968

FEBRUARY 1968:
FBI closes its investigation of the Sixteenth Street Baptist Church bombing without filing charges.

APRIL 3, 1968:
Dr. Martin Luther King Jr. delivers his "I've Been to the Mountaintop" speech in Memphis, Tennessee.

APRIL 4, 1968:
Dr. King is assassinated in Memphis.

JUNE 5, 1968:
Robert F. Kennedy is shot in Los Angeles, California, and dies 26 hours later.

1971

1971:
Alabama attorney general Bill Baxley reopens 1963 church-bombing investigation.

1977

NOVEMBER 18, 1977:
Robert Chambliss is found guilty for the murder of Denise McNair and sentenced to life in prison.

1985

OCTOBER 29, 1985:
"Dynamite Bob" Chambliss dies in prison.

1988

1988:
Alabama attorney general Don Siegelman reopens the church-bombing case again.

1989

1989:
Army general Colin Powell becomes the first black to serve as chairman of the Joint Chiefs of Staff.

1989:
L. Douglas Wilder (Virginia) becomes the first black elected governor.

1993

1993:
Birmingham-area black leaders meet with FBI about the church bombing, and agents secretly begin new review of the case.

1994

FEBRUARY 7, 1994:
Sixteenth Street Baptist Church bombing suspect Herman Frank Cash dies.

1998

OCTOBER 27, 1998:
Federal grand jury in Alabama begins hearing evidence regarding church-bombing case.

2001

APRIL 15, 2001:
Thomas Blanton Jr. goes on trial for the Sixteenth Street Baptist Church bombing.

MAY 1, 2001:
The court finds Blanton, 62, guilty on four counts of first-degree murder.

2002

MAY 6, 2002:
Carolyn testifies in court during Bobby Cherry's trial.

MAY 22, 2002:
The court finds Cherry, 71, guilty on four counts of murder and sentences him to life in prison.

2004

NOVEMBER 18, 2004:
Bobby Frank Cherry, 74, dies in prison from cancer.

2007

SPRING 2007:
Carolyn and Dr. Neal Berte raise $4 million for the Sixteenth Street Baptist Church restoration.

2008

NOVEMBER 2008:
Barack Obama is elected first African-American president of the United States.

2013

SEPTEMBER 15, 2013:
The Sixteenth Street Baptist Church will commemorate the 50th anniversary of the bombing.

CHAPTER 1

TOO GREAT A BURDEN TO BEAR

*Hate is too great a burden to bear. . . . I have decided to love. . . .
If you are seeking the highest good, I think you can find it through love.
And the beautiful thing is that we aren't moving wrong when we do it,
because John was right, God is love.*

> MARTIN LUTHER KING JR.,
> "Where Do We Go from Here?"[1]

*In the end, we will remember not the words of our enemies, but the
silence of our friends.*

> MARTIN LUTHER KING JR.

I WOKE UP ON SUNDAY MORNING, September 15, 1963, and looked out my bedroom window. The sky was slightly overcast, but the sun was trying hard to shine through the clouds. It was a warm, beautiful September day in Birmingham, Alabama—an ordinary busy Sunday morning at the Maull home.

I laid out my white Sunday dress. I had starched and ironed it before I went to bed the night before. At age fourteen, I didn't own a lot of clothes because there were six children to clothe in our household. But I had several special church dresses and one pair of black patent leather shoes I saved just for Sunday church.

Today was Youth Sunday at Sixteenth Street Baptist Church. On the fourth Sunday of each month, Reverend John H. Cross asked the church's youth to lead the service, teach the Sunday school classes, and take over jobs the adult members usually did. It proved an exciting day for us each month. The boys wore dark pants and white shirts on those Sundays, and the girls wore their prettiest white dresses.

I had been an active member of Sixteenth Street Baptist Church in Birmingham, Alabama, for as far back as I could remember. In 1950, when I was two years old, my parents registered me in the cradle-roll Sunday school class. My church served as the center of my life. I worshiped there. I socialized there. I even worked there part-time as a church secretary. Sixteenth Street Baptist Church was the first black church built in Birmingham. Since its construction in 1911, the church had become a worship home and meeting place for most of the city's black community. A host of Civil Rights leaders, including Dr. Martin Luther King Jr., had recently met there and, along with other community pastors and leaders, had planned nonviolent protests and marches. Dr. King called the Birmingham campaign Project C, with the *C* standing for "confrontation." Dr. King—and the entire black community—yearned for equal rights for blacks. Birmingham was considered the most segregated city in the South. If we could break the back of segregation in our city, it would send a strong message to the rest of the nation. But it would prove to be an extremely difficult fight.

Several responsibilities awaited me at home before I could leave for church. One of them included combing my younger sister's hair. Little Agnes had a lot of it, always uncooperative to the comb, and she had a sensitive, tender scalp. Mama herself was never good at fixing hair. At ten years of age, I started washing and pressing my own hair. I'd heat up the metal comb and run it again and again through my tangles. After Agnes came along, Mama gave me the assignment of combing her hair too. I loved taking care of Agnes and her hair, and I loved making her look pretty. It was like having my own live baby doll.

In the mornings before I left for school, Agnes usually held still and allowed me to comb and braid her hair. Even though I tried to be gentle, it usually hurt her to get the kinks out. Sometimes she'd cry. That Sunday she refused to hold still. Restless and not wanting to be bothered, she kept pushing me away.

"Please, Agnes," I begged. "Be still. I've got to be on time for Sunday school. It's Youth Sunday. I have my reports to do, and I've got to get there and count the money. I need to be on time this morning."

But my sister refused to cooperate.

"Mama," I called in desperation. "Agnes won't let me comb her hair, and I'm going to be late for Sunday school. I need to go."

"Well, just leave her here this morning," Mama told me. "You go on to church. Agnes can stay home with me."

Thank goodness! I thought. The last thing I wanted was to be late and upset Mrs. Shorter, the church secretary. She would have been working in the office and answering the phone all that morning. Mrs. Shorter and I worked side by side in the church office on Sundays.

"Come on, Wendell, Kirk!" I called to my younger brothers. "We've got to go!"

Now that my oldest brother, Samuel, was a freshman at Bradley University in Peoria, Illinois, that left my sixteen-year-old brother, Chester, as the oldest child at home. He had just gotten his driver's license, and Mama asked him to drive us to church. Chester was excited to have permission to drive the family car that morning. He sat up straight and proud behind the steering wheel of our 1960 royal blue Chevrolet Impala.

"Bring the car right back after you drop off your sister and brothers," Mama called to Chester. "Your dad needs it to drive to work."

⊕

My dad was well educated. He had earned a master's degree in applied sciences, and he taught physics and chemistry during the weekdays at the all-black George Washington Carver High School in North Birmingham. Prior to that, Daddy had taught at Industrial High School, which later became A. H. Parker High School—the first high school in Birmingham built specifically for black students. In the evenings and on weekends, in spite of his intelligence and education, he worked a menial job. He waited tables at the elite, white-members-only Birmingham Country Club in prestigious Mountain Brook, a city with old money and deeply ingrained segregated ways. It proved a lowly position for Daddy, but he did what he needed to do to feed his family and keep the roof over our heads. He couldn't eat at the Birmingham Country Club, of course—people of color couldn't. But they worked there cooking, serving, and cleaning up. My parents had dreams that each of their children would graduate from college, so Dad earmarked the money from this job for college savings for the six of us kids.

Before Daddy left home in the evenings and on weekends, he'd slip into the club's waiter uniform, a short white jacket trimmed in green cord around the sleeves and neck, with *BCC* embroidered on the front. After he arrived, he would pull on freshly bleached waiter's gloves and begin his work. My father would occasionally speak to us about his experiences and interactions with the customers at the BCC. He did his job well, responded with the mandatory "Yes, Sir" to diners' demands, and pretty much just kept his mouth shut. He never spoke about his education or teaching position while he was there, not wanting his employers or customers to call him uppity and take away his job.

Daddy never told us what he overheard around the country club tables he served. I guess he didn't want to frighten us—he always tried hard to protect us. He wasn't alone in his approach. In those days, adults in the black community didn't talk to their children about painful happenings. They just kept quiet about those things and tried to move on, in spite of all that was going on around them. But I have no doubt that during the thirty years he worked there, he learned much about racist Birmingham. I suspect he occasionally heard conversations from Klan club members that caused his heart to miss a beat. But when such remarks caused him additional fears and concerns, he just enforced new rules upon his children—hard-to-follow, strict rules. He was very much a disciplinarian, and he regimented our coming and going. He expected complete obedience to whatever rules he laid down at home. We understood, and we usually obeyed to the letter. If we decided not to listen, we knew harsh punishment would follow. It was years before we realized that his unwieldy rules were designed to protect us from the evil possibilities of the mean-spirited world around us.

"You children aren't to go near the railroad tracks going toward the pipe company," Daddy ordered us. He gave no reason. He didn't have to. As strict as he was, we knew Daddy was just and fair. We knew he loved us and wanted what was best for us.

Daddy often warned my older brothers, "Samuel and Chester, you protect our 'girl-child' and walk to school together." Daddy rarely called me by my name, Carolyn. He referred to me as the family's "girl-child" or "Caroline." It wasn't uncommon to hear Daddy demand, "If three children leave this house together, then three children must return to this house together!" We had to know where each sibling was at all times. We were definitely our "brothers' keepers."

As Birmingham grew increasingly violent in the 1960s, Daddy's list of nonnegotiable rules grew longer from year to year. We knew he meant business, and we knew better than to question him. I sulked when Daddy insisted that I, his girl-child, be escorted almost everywhere I went. I didn't mind so much when my older brothers walked with me down the streets of Birmingham or accompanied me to neighborhood parties. But I felt terribly embarrassed when Daddy made my two younger brothers go with me. Because of Daddy's tight leash, I also wasn't allowed to spend the night at any of my friends' homes or babysit for children in the community. About the only place he permitted me to go alone, unescorted by my brothers, was church. It was a safe place, and I had certain responsibilities there. I escaped to the church as often as I could.

When we occasionally disobeyed a rule, Daddy enforced punishment that we would long remember. Sometimes he grounded us or put us in temporary isolation if we got out of line. The boys got their share of spankings, but my father hardly ever spanked me. Instead, he'd take away Sunday afternoon movie privileges or not let me talk on the phone or tell me I couldn't go to club meetings with my friends. He believed discipline and rules were a must for children, especially young boys—and especially those growing up in Birmingham, Alabama.

Daddy also imposed a five-minute limit on the use of the bathroom and the telephone. If we exceeded our five minutes, particularly if someone else was waiting to use the phone, Daddy simply unplugged it. He also made strict rules about hitting a girl-child. My brothers knew not to hit me or my little sister because if they did, they could expect to be in a lot of trouble. Daddy believed in respecting and protecting women. We knew we needed to show Mama utmost respect—showing Mama disrespect always, without fail, meant severe punishment. If my dad thought we had even looked at my mother in a disrespectful way, we faced big trouble.

Sometimes we unwisely tested Daddy's rules. One day when Chester was fifteen, with a learner's permit but no license, he slipped away with the family car. According to reports from the neighbors, boys ran alongside the car, holding onto the door handles from the outside, while my brother drove really fast. But in the course of this showing off, one of his buddies fell to the ground and ended up scraped and scratched. Soon enough the boy's father paid Daddy a visit. My dad became really angry, and he not only whipped Chester but took away his learner's permit for three whole months. Chester learned his lesson. He never did that again!

Wendell, my mischievous brother, was always in trouble. Daddy enrolled Wendell in the ninth grade class at Carver High School, where he worked, even though it lay outside our school zone. For the sake of convenience, teachers were allowed to enroll their children where they taught. But Daddy had an additional reason for wanting him there.

"I can keep an eye on this boy if I take him with me," Daddy said.

I remember when Wendell, shortly before his high school graduation, grew a little beard on the bottom of his chin— just a few hairs that formed a goatee. But Carver High School said it wouldn't graduate any student who had hair on his face.

On graduation morning Wendell decided to be clever. He put Band-Aids over his chin hair and told his teachers, "I cut my chin when I shaved off the hair."

As far as the school was concerned, he had gotten away with it, and he graduated with his class—and his Band-Aids. But he didn't fool Daddy. Not a bit. Daddy was so upset with Wendell he wrote a letter to the dean at Knoxville College, where Wendell had been accepted for the coming fall.

"It appears that I have not yet taught my son the meaning of character and integrity," Daddy wrote. "He has not learned to be a responsible member of society. For this reason, I am canceling Wendell's acceptance to attend your college in the fall semester."

Wendell was shocked when he read the letter. He begged Daddy to reconsider, but my father refused. Wendell had to be punished.

Daddy never mailed the letter, even though he made Wendell believe he had. Later, a month before the fall semester was to begin, Daddy pretended to have changed his mind and told Wendell he could attend after all. But for most of the summer, my brother thought all his friends would go without him to Knoxville College, and he would have to get a job and stay home. It was quite a lesson.

When we entered high school, my father would make us take the same tests he prepared for his high school students. He worked us hard. If he didn't like our grades on his tests, he made us study and retake the tests until we made better grades. His rules proved a real source of aggravation for me. I thought we had the strictest father in town.

Daddy liked things organized and efficient—a place for everything and everything in its place. He knew where things were: socks in the top dresser drawers, toys in the bedroom closets, skates and bikes on the back porch, and pots and pans stacked neatly in the kitchen cabinet. He arranged the kitchen in a certain way, and he made sure we put things back in their designated places. No doubt these habits were a carryover from his mother, whose name was Sweet. She died when my dad was sixteen, but in that relatively short amount of time she taught him to cook, sew, iron, and make his bed. Sweet was not formally educated, but she trained Dad well in the practical aspects of life. Daddy's time in the U.S. Army no doubt influenced his orderly lifestyle too. As an Army cook, he'd learned to live a strictly regimented routine. It wasn't unusual for Daddy to wake us up at three or four in the morning after he got off work at the BCC and walk us to the kitchen to look at what we'd failed to clean properly before bedtime.

He'd stand us all in front of the kitchen counter and ask, "Whose week was it to do the dishes?" After he determined who was responsible, he'd point to the less-than-perfect kitchen and ask, "What's wrong with this picture? What didn't you do here?"

Before the guilty child could return to bed and go back to sleep, Daddy made him or her scrub down the kitchen—as he or she should have done earlier. Daddy insisted that the kitchen be clean and ready for his use in the morning. He had enough challenges each morning—waking us, feeding us, and making certain he arrived at work on time. After a long night of working at the club, he saw no reason why he should have to come home to a dirty kitchen.

Early in their marriage, Daddy and Mama created a special arrangement involving family responsibilities. Daddy cooked breakfast every morning for the family, and Mama cooked supper each evening after she got home from her school-teaching job. Mama proved just the opposite from efficient, organized Daddy. She had a laid-back, unassuming personality. Totally unorganized, she didn't care if we never washed the dishes in the kitchen sink. Nothing upset her. The house could burn down around her, and I don't think she'd pay much attention to it. I guess Daddy knew that if he didn't establish some order and organization in a house with six growing children, chaos would rule.

✦

As Chester drove Wendell, Kirk, and me to church that fateful Sunday, I thought about my best friend, Cynthia Wesley. Her father had been my elementary school principal at Finley Avenue Elementary School, and Cynthia and I were in the same Sunday school class. We talked on the phone almost every day, and we were both members of a small all-girl community club called the Cavalettes. The group of about fifteen black Cavalettes got together mostly to socialize, eat cookies, drink punch, talk, and dance to records we played on the portable record player. We had just had a club meeting the week before, and we had another one scheduled for the afternoon of Sunday, September 15. The upcoming meeting would be particularly exciting for us because we had placed an article in the local newspaper about it. The announcement simply said, "Cavalette Club to meet Sept. 15 at 3 p.m." I served as our president, and I had told everyone to bring three dollars that Sunday to pay for the matching gold caps and shirts we had ordered from Fred Singleton's, the downtown Birmingham sporting-goods store. Our first names would be printed in black letters on the front of the shirts, and the letter *C* for Cavalettes would be printed on the back. We could hardly wait to get them the following week.

The Wesleys had adopted their only child, Cynthia. They lived in a beautiful brick house in Smithfield, an area of Birmingham better known as "Dynamite Hill" because of the routine Klan bombings there. Back in 1948, the year I was born, several black families had crossed the "color line" that separated white homes from black homes in the Smithfield area of Birmingham. The Klan responded with random bombings for almost two decades. Several well-known Civil Rights activists lived in Dynamite Hill at the time, including Angela Davis, whose family had a house at the top of the hill on Center Street, and Arthur Shores, one of the first blacks to practice law in Alabama. The Klan bombed the Shoreses' brick ranch house on two different occasions. Fortunately, neither he nor his family was injured either time.

I wondered what Cynthia would wear on that Youth Sunday. Her mother sewed all her clothes because she could never find anything to fit Cynthia's petite size-two frame. Mrs. Wesley made beautiful clothes for her daughter— dresses just the right length and color and that perfectly fit Cynthia's tiny waist.

Chester pulled the car to the side of the street in front of the church. My little brothers and I stepped out of the car and walked into the church's lower-level door, which opened to the basement. The children's Sunday school classes met each Sunday in the lower auditorium. The adult Sunday school classes met upstairs—each one in a corner of the large main sanctuary or in the balcony between the two great stained-glass windows. In one window, Jesus tenderly held a lamb in his strong arms. I sometimes pictured myself as that little lamb, so safe and secure and loved in my Shepherd's hands. In the other window, my favorite one, was the kind-faced Jesus, poised with his hand in front of a large wooden door. I could almost hear him knocking softly, respectfully, on the door . . . again and again and again. His face showed a tender pleading for the person inside to open the door and let him in. I came to learn that the door represented a lost person's heart—a heart Jesus longed to enter and live within. I studied those windows closely every Sunday, and each one permanently etched itself in my mind. On both sides of the sanctuary, the stained-glassed images of Jesus comforted me and brought me great peace and joy.

The children's Sunday school classes were already in session when I sat both boys in their metal folding chairs. I walked upstairs to the church office and found middle-aged Mabel Shorter unusually flustered as she laid down the telephone receiver.

"What's wrong, Mrs. Shorter?"

"All these phone calls!" she said. "People have been ringing the phone all morning. But when I try to get more information, they just hang up."

"Who are they? What do they want?" I asked.

"Oh, I don't know," she said. "But they seem more like *threatening* calls than just *prankster* calls. The callers say they are going to bomb the church."

Mrs. Shorter was the nervous type. I felt she might be overreacting, so I mentally dismissed her comments.

I didn't think any more about the threatening phone calls. I just felt so proud Reverend Cross had asked me to be the Sunday school secretary on Sunday mornings. I'd held this job since the seventh grade. I would man the office, listen for the phone, open the week's mail, greet guests when they came through, and compile the morning's Sunday school report. I would also record the attendance and the amount of money contributed to church that morning. I felt so grown up.

After the Sunday school lesson, the classes would all gather together in a large assembly before the morning service began. I would read the report summary out loud to everyone and make some necessary announcements before the superintendent dismissed everyone at 10:45. During those fifteen minutes before the next worship service, church folk would talk with one another, admire the babies, purposefully compliment and encourage the youth, and visit the restrooms.

My friends and I would slip out of the church between Sunday school and the 11:00 a.m. worship service to drink Cokes at Mr. Gaston's motel restaurant. This was a black-owned restaurant, the only place in the area that served blacks and allowed us to sit in a booth and have a waitress bring us a cold drink. We felt so grown up when we sat at a table; said, "Coca-Cola, please"; and waited for our drinks. We would each pay our thirty-five cents and then hurry back to the church.

Some nine years before, Mr. Arthur George Gaston, the grandson of slaves and a popular self-made millionaire, had built the A. G. Gaston Motel on the edge of Kelly Ingram Park—across the street from the church—on some land he had bought years earlier. The motel provided a place for black Civil Rights leaders to stay, as well as other visitors to the city. No other motel in Birmingham would allow black visitors to eat or sleep there. Before the A. G. Gaston Motel opened, they had to stay in the homes of church members. Mr. Gaston hung a large Z-shaped sign from the top of the two-story part of the brick building. It read simply,

A. G. Gaston MOTEL
Air-Conditioned

Before long, Daddy found out about our visits to the Gaston Motel restaurant, and he put an abrupt stop to them.

"When you go to church," Daddy said, "you stay at church until you leave to go home."

It was just another rule he added to the already long list of restrictions. So I didn't leave church anymore and order Coca-Colas at the Gaston Motel.

⊕

I left the flustered Mrs. Shorter in the church office, distributed record books to each of the Sunday school classes, and then quietly slipped into my own classroom. Around 10:20, after I had collected all the children's records, I headed toward the steps leading to the sanctuary to collect the adult Sunday school records. I paused and lingered a minute at the door to the girls' restroom.

"Hey! Good morning!" I called to four of my friends who were primping in front of the restroom's large lounge mirror. At that time, I didn't know that *five* girls were in the bathroom. I didn't see Sarah, Addie's sister, who was in a separate area near the washbowls and toilets.

The four girls—Denise, Addie, Carole, and Cynthia—combed their hair and chattered excitedly as they readied themselves for the 11:00 morning youth service.

Denise McNair smiled at me. She was always smiling, showing that little gap between her two front teeth. One of our teachers told us that in Africa "the gap" was considered a rare and enviable beauty mark. At eleven years old, Denise was a few years younger than I was, but I thought she was pretty and smart, and I always liked the way her mom fixed her hair.

An only child, Denise was doted on by her parents and grandparents. She always wore pretty, dainty clothes—dresses with fluffy matching pinafores. Denise's father, Mr. McNair, was my ninth grade teacher. He taught diversified education at Parker High School on Fourth Avenue North in Birmingham. An accomplished photographer, he also owned a black portrait studio. Mrs. McNair, Denise's mother, had a beautiful voice and sang in the church choir. Sometimes

Denise sat beside her mother up in the loft during worship services.

Poised at the bathroom mirror next to Denise was Addie Collins, a sweet, quiet girl. I liked Addie, but we weren't particularly close buddies. Addie was just kind of *there*—serious and serene. She never fussed with anybody or said anything mean. I was closer to Addie's sister, Junie—I just seemed to gravitate toward her. A little mischievous, Junie laughed a lot and was always so much fun. Junie told me later that she and Addie had argued on the way to church that morning.

Carole Robertson glanced up and smiled at me too. Our mothers both taught school and were good friends. Carole, a member of Girl Scout troop #264, pinned the numerous badges she had earned to a long sash that draped across her chest and proudly wore her uniform to school. She was cute and always looked impressive in her uniform and badges. Carole played the clarinet in the school band. She was supposed to play that next night—Monday—at Parker High School's first football game of the year.

Carole loved God and church as much as I did. We'd grown up together in the church, attending the Easter egg hunts as children and later participating side by side in the youth programs. Carole carried a small Bible in her pocket whenever she went to church and was involved in most of the Sixteenth Street programs, usually with a speaking part. Though she lived in a segregated city with few opportunities for girls of our race, Carole found all kinds of things to do to keep busy. She seemed to hate just sitting still and was always on the move. Mature and ladylike at just fourteen years old, she was a person on a mission: she seemed to know exactly where she was going in life, with a sort of inward direction driving her. I imagined that Carole would become the president of something when she grew up or a leader such as Dorothy Height or Mary McLeod Bethune.

My best friend, Cynthia Wesley, also stood at the mirror in the basement restroom. I loved Cynthia and her family. She had a great sense of humor, made jokes, and laughed all the time. Her father, Claude Wesley, had been my principal at Finley Avenue Elementary School. That day the Reverend had asked Cynthia to be an usher. She stood at the mirror adjusting the handmade dress that perfectly hugged her tiny waist.

The Wesleys were professional people, prim and proper, but not in a stuck-up way. I think Mrs. Wesley had had throat cancer years before, although I'm not sure. No black person I knew would ever say the word *cancer*. When someone slipped and said "the word," a dark, evil cloud seemed to settle over the room, and everyone started feeling uncomfortable. After Mrs. Wesley's surgery, she wore some sort of voice box with a small microphone attached. She wrapped pretty scarves around her neck to hide the box, and somehow these scarves always matched her beautiful outfits. But I could hear it when she spoke—the raspy breathing, the gathered mucus, the slightly mechanical tone.

I remember the way Mr. Wesley walked into my classroom at school—so proper and organized, but not intimidating.

He wanted everything to be just right, much like my father did. He never commented on the racial slurs scribbled on the pages of the used textbooks the white schools gave us when they received new ones. Instead, he poured his energy into the positives. When I won the city, county, and state spelling competitions organized for black students, Mr. Wesley publicly expressed a special pride in me.

The Wesleys' home was neat, orderly, and beautiful. Mrs. Wesley made their drapes, and she made sure their hardwood floors sparkled. We had many of our Cavalettes meetings at the Wesleys' home on Dynamite Hill.

In later years, after the bombing, Mrs. Wesley often reflected on her last conversation with Cynthia on September 15. "That morning," she told me, "Cynthia walked out the front door, and I called her back into the house. 'Little lady,' I said, 'is that your slip I see showing below your dress?' A bit of slip lace hung longer than her dress. I suggested she change it before she left for church."

⊕

I left the girls in the restroom. "See you later!" I called and started up the stairs.

I hurried because the reports had to be summarized by 10:30, when the classes reconvened and the superintendent would stand up and announce, "Sister Maull will read today's Sunday school summary for us."

As I ran up the stairs, I heard the phone ringing in the

church office. Out of breath, I rushed inside, picked up the heavy black receiver, and put it to my ear. I opened my mouth to say hello, but before I could say anything, a male voice said simply, "Three minutes."

Then he hung up.

CHAPTER 2

HALFWAY IN AND HALFWAY OUT

Nineteen sixty-three is not an end, but a beginning.

DR. MARTIN LUTHER KING JR.,
"I Have a Dream" [1]

*All of us might wish at times that we lived in a more tranquil world,
but we don't. And if our times are difficult and perplexing, so are they
challenging and filled with opportunity.*

ROBERT F. KENNEDY

I OFTEN TELL PEOPLE I was born in Birmingham, halfway in and halfway out of the South's violent Civil Rights era. As a young teen, I lived in North Birmingham (near ACIPCO, the American Cast Iron Pipe Company) during the city's (and the nation's) darkest and most difficult days—at its worst, when segregation laws proved the fiercest. And I still lived there when those laws came tumbling down. I measured my life in two distinct segments: BB (before the bombing) and AB (after the bombing). I lived through some of the nation's worst atrocities. But I also witnessed the beginning of healing and forgiveness.

Not many young people can pinpoint the exact date, time, and place they grew up and became an adult. I can. It was September 15, 1963, 10:22 a.m., at the Sixteenth Street Baptist Church in Birmingham, Alabama. My life changed forever after that day. Not only did I lose four friends, but I also lost my innocence and naiveté about people and about the world in general. The loving trust I had in the goodness of humanity was gone. I began to see the world as a deadly and hostile place, where no one, not even my father or my brothers or my church, could protect me. And for the first time in my life, I felt all alone.

⊕

My mother, Ernestine Burt Maull, gave birth to me, her third child and first girl-child, three years after World War II ended—on January 13, 1948. I was born in my grandfather's house in Clanton, Alabama, a city about sixty miles south of North Birmingham. Most black babies were born at home in those days—rarely in hospitals. Daddy often bragged that he helped deliver me. Although he never told me specifically what his role was, I suspect he probably assisted by boiling water and supplying fresh towels. No doubt he also was my mother's encourager.

My parents moved to Birmingham when I was two years old, and there I came face-to-face with Jim Crow laws, which enforced segregation. These laws resulted in inferior accommodations for blacks and served only to fuel the existing fear and hatred between blacks and whites.

Fear proved a way of life for most people of color in the Deep South during the post–World War II era. But as a child, I felt protected and safe from harm. I lived in a climate of relative security—if you don't consider the Klan's random bombings in my area—until more visible signs of unrest and change came to Birmingham in the early sixties. As long as we obeyed the enforced Jim Crow laws and kept our mouths shut, things were bearable. My family and neighbors never challenged the status quo. We had too much to lose—none of us wanted to risk our jobs or our lives.

Living black carried with it certain rules, and there were dire consequences if those rules were broken. Blacks who rode a city bus paid their money in the front of the bus but entered and got off the bus through the back door. They sat in the rear seats behind the signs that said "coloreds." We were careful not to use public toilets or to drink from

FROM MARTIN LUTHER KING JR.'S "I HAVE A DREAM" SPEECH

Five score years ago, a great American, in whose symbolic shadow we stand signed the Emancipation Proclamation. This momentous decree came as a great beacon light of hope to millions of Negro slaves who had been seared in the flames of withering injustice. It came as a joyous daybreak to end the long night of captivity.

But one hundred years later, we must face the tragic fact that the Negro is still not free. One hundred years later, the life of the Negro is still sadly crippled by the manacles of segregation and the chains of discrimination. One hundred years later, the Negro lives on a lonely island of poverty in the midst of a vast ocean of material prosperity. One hundred years later, the Negro is still languishing in the corners of American society and finds himself an exile in his own land. So we have come here today to dramatize an appalling condition. . . .

It would be fatal for the nation to overlook the urgency of the moment and to underestimate the determination of the Negro. This sweltering summer of the Negro's legitimate discontent will not pass until there is an invigorating autumn of freedom and equality. Nineteen sixty-three is not an end, but a beginning. Those who hope that the Negro needed to blow off steam and will now be content will have a rude awakening if the nation returns to business as usual. There will be neither rest nor tranquility in America until the Negro is granted his citizenship rights. The whirlwinds of revolt will continue to shake the foundations of our nation until the bright day of justice emerges.[2]

water fountains marked "whites only." When we traveled by car to visit relatives in other cities, we made sure everyone went to the bathroom before we left. And since many restaurants in the South didn't allow blacks to eat there (some even had signs in the windows that said "We serve no Negroes, Mexicans, or dogs"), we packed our lunches and had picnics on the roadside instead. We always tried to arrive at our destination long before dark because no motels would allow us to stay there and also for safety reasons: it was not uncommon for cars with black passengers inside to be attacked when traveling after dark. So if we had to drive at night, we were mindful of the speed limit, lest we get stopped by white police.

The summer I was twelve, I traveled to Ohio with my mother's sister, who lived in Columbus. My aunt had asked me to go to Ohio with her so I could babysit her children. At one point during the trip I told her I had to go to the bathroom. She stopped the car on the side of the road.

"See that house down there, Carolyn?" she said. "Those look like good people. Go and ask them if you can use their bathroom."

I looked down the road and saw a house far in the distance. "I could never do that! Anyway, I'm afraid to go down there!"

No doubt rural blacks at that time were accustomed to strangers stopping at their house to use the bathroom. But this was new to me—and unimaginable. When I refused to walk to the house, my aunt said, "Well, Carolyn, you've got two choices: either go down to that house and ask to use the bathroom, or go behind the car and do your business."

So while my aunt waited, I squatted down behind her car, praying that no one would drive by and see me "doing my business."

⊕

Despite the occasional bombings in my city and the Jim Crow laws that were part of my daily reality, I felt safe as a child. I had my family, and I had my church—the strong, seemingly impenetrable, brick building that sat like a fortress on the corner of Sixteenth Street and Sixth Avenue for as long as I could remember. When I wasn't at home or in school or at Cynthia's house meeting with the Cavalettes, my parents knew I was at church. Even Daddy could rest assured that I'd be safe there; getting hurt just wasn't something you thought about happening at church.

At that time our church served as a concert hall, a public auditorium, and the gathering place for most African-American social events. Church really was everything to us. And Sixteenth Street Baptist Church had its own rich history long before landmark Civil Rights events thrust it into the public eye.

Some of my fondest memories as a youngster were from my times at church. Sometimes I'd sit quietly in the sanctuary when it was empty and just look around. I knew all the nooks and crannies, the hidden door that led from the balcony, the "secret room" where my friends and I met to talk. As a little girl, I'd played all over the building—even up in the balcony and in the choir loft. I never missed the annual Easter egg hunt held at Kelly Ingram Park or vacation Bible school, which was held for two weeks every summer. Our church placed high value on its children, and I was there in the middle of every opportunity that was offered.

I'll never forget my baptism one Sunday morning in September 1961. The previous week, after listening to the music and the reverend's sermon, I had walked to the front of the church during the altar call. *I want to be like Jesus*, I was thinking as I went forward. On the Sunday I was baptized, Reverend John Cross dipped me deep into the church's pool of warm baptismal water. When he lifted me up, I opened my eyes, blinked back the water, and immediately looked up into Jesus' stained-glass face on the large window just in front of me. Jesus' eyes had an inviting look, a calm demeanor, a divine patience as he stood outside the wooden door and knocked. I saw in his face a safety and protection beyond anything I could imagine in my small world. "Dead, buried, resurrected with Christ," Reverend said as he baptized me. I had just placed myself under the protection of Christ, and I could almost hear Jesus saying from that window, "Carolyn, I'm here, watching over you." For more than half a century, the kind face of Jesus had looked down on its worshipers at Sixteenth Street Baptist Church and had offered them that same security.

My family's entire social life revolved around the church.

In fact, life at home seemed kind of boring compared to life at church. My brothers did their best to make me miserable, as brothers are inclined to do at times. They'd tell me—the girl-child—to get lost whenever their friends came over. They wanted to play only with boys, and they made it clear that in their minds it was a *mistake* that a girl had entered the Maull family. They might not have wanted me around, but at church I always felt accepted and loved. Nobody there cared that I was a girl-child. Every week I waited for Sunday to roll around the way most kids wait for Christmas.

The reverend gave me responsibilities at church that made me feel mature and important. I worked in the church office whenever I could. Reverend Cross knew I had been raised and trained in the church and that I was familiar with church business and program planning. He also knew my grandfather, Reverend Ernest Walter Burt. One of fourteen children, my grandfather served as pastor of two churches south of Birmingham. One Sunday he would preach at Macedonia Baptist Church in Columbiana, and the next week he'd be at Beulah Baptist Church in Thorsby. He was also secretary of the National Baptist Convention, and by the time he passed in the spring of 1971, he had served as a principal and teacher in the Chilton County School System for four decades.

I loved visiting my grandfather and my grandmother, "Mama Lessie." It was worth sitting through a long sermon knowing a feast awaited us on the tables outside the church. The menu was always the same: fried chicken, collard greens, potato salad, boiled okra, sliced tomatoes, corn bread, and chocolate or coconut cake. Both Granddaddy and Mama Lessie taught me some rock-solid church organizational skills that proved good training for my work at Sixteenth Street Baptist Church.

One year when I was in high school, Reverend Cross asked me to represent our church at the National Baptist Convention in Tulsa, Oklahoma. I felt so honored. While in Tulsa, I walked through the hallways of Oral Roberts University and noticed that many of the buildings were made of glass. I watched the students walk back and forth to class. *What a beautiful campus*, I thought. *I wish I could see Oral Roberts himself.* I had seen him on television, and I longed to meet him in person. As I walked around the campus, this thought came to mind: *How wonderful it would be to go to a university like this! I feel so comfortable here. I wish the University of Alabama welcomed black students and made them feel as comfortable as I feel here.*

A decade earlier, on May 17, 1954, in the *Brown v. Board of Education* decision, the United States Supreme Court overruled the "separate but equal" laws once adopted in the 1896 *Plessy v. Ferguson* case. The Court had decided that "segregation of white and Negro children in the public schools of a State solely on the basis of race . . . denies to Negro children the equal protection of the laws guaranteed by the Fourteenth Amendment." Chief Justice Earl Warren stated, "Segregation of white and colored children in public schools has a detrimental effect upon the colored children . . . for the policy of separating the races is usually interpreted as denoting the inferiority of the negro group."[3] Warren ordered the nation's public schools to desegregate "with all deliberate speed."

But the state of Alabama chose not to cooperate with the Supreme Court decision. Alabama's public schools and facilities remained strictly segregated. Powerful white men—state and city leaders, as well as the Klan-infiltrated police department—used intimidation and bombs to keep blacks and whites separated. Segregation was also enforced by law, and a breach could result in fines or time spent in jail. Governor Wallace was one of the state's most vocal proponents of segregation, and the way things were going, it seemed that nothing and no one would be able to prevail against him.

Unless things changed within the next few years, when it came time for me to choose a college, I felt sure I would be confronting Governor Wallace himself, as he personally barred the front door of any all-white state university in Alabama.

⊕

As a youth, I spent as much time in the church library as I could, especially since blacks weren't allowed to use the Birmingham Public Library. I often manned the church library, checking out books to members, stamping the due dates on the cards inside, and making sure the borrowed books were returned on time. During the slow times I sat in the quiet room and read books about our church's history. Dr. Charles Brown, our unofficial church historian, had recorded stories about the church and had compiled photos taken throughout its many years. As an educator and a teacher, Dr. Brown loved history, and he somehow sensed that these records from the first black church in Birmingham would be significant someday. I devoured those history books. The church library sparked a love in me for reading at home, too. I enjoyed reading the encyclopedias Mama had bought us. One day I read through the *S* volume, another day through *L*. Granddaddy had given me *The Prayers of Peter Marshall*, and I read it again and again. It proved to be my favorite book. I still use those prayers today.

One year Sixteenth Street Baptist Church formed a church tennis team. I immediately joined. Miss Effie Jewett McCaw, a single woman who taught school and later became a principal, served as our first tennis coach. The YMCA on Eighteenth Street South, although segregated, allowed us to practice on its tennis court. My tennis partner, Richard Young, and I, as well as other church youth, took tennis lessons there from Miss Effie.

Miss Effie loved the church children. A woman full of fun and life, she sat in the back pews of the Sixteenth Street Baptist Church congregation on Sunday mornings and whistled the hymns while everybody else sang them. She reminded me of a little canary back there, her gentle whistle rising above the voices, organ, and piano. I have never known anyone since who could rival her "gift of whistle." I adored Miss Effie. She never married or had children of her own; maybe that's why she took such a genuine interest in us.

I also looked up to Mr. John T. Smith, another church member at Sixteenth Street Baptist Church. Mr. Smith managed the public swimming pools in Leeds, Alabama, a small city about twenty miles east of downtown Birmingham. At that time, swimming pools, like everything else, were designated "whites only" or "coloreds." Rather than fight the desegregation battle, Birmingham closed all its downtown city pools—both black and white. Even Memorial Park on the south side closed its "all black" pool, so during the hot, steamy Birmingham summers, children had no place to swim.

The whites-only swimming pool in Leeds remained open during those long, hot days when most neighboring cities had closed their public pools. For one week in June and the last week in August, Mr. Smith, the pool's black caretaker, closed the Leeds pool for cleaning, maintenance, and repairs. During those weeks, the church filled up its bus with children and drove us to the Leeds pool, where Mr. Smith met us and allowed us to swim. We'd arrive at the pool around nine o'clock in the morning and stay till four o'clock in the afternoon. Church mothers packed a bunch of food for us to eat—sandwiches, chicken, fruit, and cold drinks. Moms sat on the edge of the pool while their youngsters splashed and played in the cool water, keeping a close eye to make sure no youngsters drowned. The adults from church took every opportunity to encourage and compliment us. I can still hear them happily calling to us, "Oh! You do such a good job diving off the high diving board!" "Why look, Carolyn's not afraid to jump off."

I often wondered about Mr. Smith and "his" swimming pool. *Do the white people of Leeds know that colored children from downtown Birmingham are splashing around in their swimming pool? Did Mr. Smith get special permission for us to use the pool those weeks?* I'll probably never know, but some of my most wonderful summertime memories happened at the "whites only" swimming pool in Leeds, Alabama.

As a child and youth, I had little contact with white people. Sometimes a white inspector came to our school and filled out a report sheet, or I might see white department store clerks when we bought various items. But it wasn't until I went to college that I actually had a conversation and interaction with a white person. Blacks and whites lived together in the same city, but we truly lived in *separate* worlds. As Eugene "Bull" Connor said in one of his classic malapropisms, "White and Negro are not to segregate together."[4] I never questioned the Birmingham laws that illegally enforced segregation of public facilities—facilities that both black and white citizens paid tax dollars to build and support.

In reality, I was much more aware of places that were off-limits by Daddy's orders than by state mandate. Daddy made sure we obeyed his rules, but I don't remember his ever speaking about Birmingham's Segregation Racial Ordinances, let alone bringing a copy into the house. His strict rules were designed as an invisible form of protection for us, and in many ways they reflected Birmingham's segregation laws. For instance, he wouldn't let us ride the city bus. We did ride the school bus, but if the six of us needed to go anywhere else, either Mama or Daddy drove us.

Daddy told us never to cross the railroad tracks that led into North Birmingham. He gave us no reason, but he no doubt knew that Klan members such as Robert Chambliss and Bob Cherry lived in that part of town. I always suspected that Daddy, as an "invisible" waiter, learned more at the Birmingham Country Club about Klan activities than he ever wanted to know.

When Mama took us to the bargain basement sales in the Loveman's and Pizitz department stores, we never asked why we couldn't try on clothes. Mama would hold up a pair of jeans marked "irregular" to a brother's hips and try to ensure that each pair had enough leg length to last through the whole school year. She knew she couldn't return the jeans if they didn't fit. When we walked into Pizitz, we could smell the food and see the grand spiral staircase that led to the whites-only mezzanine café. We watched white people eating in the mezzanine, but we never asked why we couldn't go up those stairs. It was just the way things were.

Mama became acquainted with a kindhearted white woman who worked at the Parisian Shoe Store in downtown Birmingham. Mama watched for the sales and then gathered all us children every so often to buy shoes there. The salesclerk allowed my brothers, my sister, and me to actually *try on* new Sunday shoes, as well as Hush Puppies and penny loafers for school, before we bought them. When we went shoe shopping at Parisian's, Mama packed each one of us a freshly laundered pair of white socks. The white woman purposefully watched Mama take off our socks and slip a clean pair on our feet before we tried on the shoes.

When the new Jack's fast-food restaurant opened near our home, we begged to go there to buy French fries. My greatest desire was to walk into Jack's, sit down at the lunch counter, and order French fries with ketchup. Mama never told us that only white children could do that. She just said, "Children, we don't have money to spend on French fries! I can buy a week's worth of groceries for what we'd pay for those fries!" We took her at her word, and we hushed about it.

During those days I didn't think much about the signs that hung above water fountains, toilets, bus station waiting rooms, restaurants, theaters, and other public places. The truth is, our parents kept us close to home so we would have minimum exposure to the signs and to white people. By the time I could read, I learned I could use any things or places marked "coloreds," and I could not use those things or places marked "whites only." What I had not yet learned was the depth of hatred that mandated those segregation laws. It seemed that what people learned at their churches on Sundays about unity and love they placed on the shelf during the remainder of the week. We were engaged in a no-win hate war. But as long as we black people "stayed in our places," our community was relatively safe.

One day while my mother shopped at Pizitz during a bargain basement sale, my little brother, Kirk, stood on his tiptoes and drank from a whites-only water fountain. A white man approached Kirk and told him he could not drink water from that particular fountain. My mother overheard the scolding and stood up to the man. "He can't read the 'whites only' sign," she said. "He's only five years old!"

I was aware of the signs, but my family never talked about them. I didn't feel angry or inferior because I had to use the toilets that were marked "coloreds." Not until Dr. Martin Luther King Jr. came to our church and called the signs and other inequalities to our attention did I really start to notice them and their underlying message. Dr. King pointed to the drinking fountains and said, "See these signs? They shouldn't be here. These are the things we're trying to change." Dr. King told us that we ought to be able to use the public water fountains in the city because "all water is God's water." I couldn't have understood at the time that the signs were symbolic—and symptomatic—of deeper issues within our society. I would soon have a rude and painful awakening.

Being born halfway in and halfway out of the Civil Rights movement, I had questions: Was it an advantage or a disadvantage? Did God intend for me to be in the middle of the vicious struggle between blacks and whites during the 1960s? And if so, for what reason? At the time I couldn't see any blessing in those closed doors, but in the years since, I have learned that God makes no mistakes. All the things that happened to me were working together for good. I was caught in a particular moment of national history, smack in the middle of a city known as the nation's hotbed of racial injustice and violence. But even as young as I was, I felt that God was watching and that he would, indeed, bring good out of this situation. No matter how bleak things looked to me, I trusted God to work this out for the good of my community. I had to trust.

In the midst of everything, I had a strong fortress, a refuge from the violent world around me—Sixteenth Street Baptist Church, the sanctuary where I could freely worship God and find peace, safety, and security within its strong, comforting, brick walls. And I had the stained-glass face of Jesus in the window looking down upon me with his love, approval, and assurance of protection against the hostile world outside.

That is, until the morning of September 15, 1963.

CHAPTER 3

THE STRONG ONE

※

Carolyn . . . your name means "strong one." Whenever you are called by your name, Carolyn, *the person is also calling into your life the strength you own through your name.*

MY GRANDFATHER, REVEREND DR. ERNEST WALTER BURT

Few will have the greatness to bend history itself, but each of us can work to change a small portion of events, and in the total of all those acts will be written the history of this generation.

ROBERT F. KENNEDY

"Three minutes," the mysterious caller had said. As I placed the receiver back in its cradle, I pondered the call for a few seconds. Then I remembered I had not yet collected the adult Sunday school reports.

⊕

I took seriously my responsibilities at church. Reverend had entrusted me with adult-size jobs, and my grandfather had instilled within me long ago a deep sense of sacred honor in doing God's work. My grandfather's confidence in my abilities made me hold my head a little higher. Whenever my grandfather came to Birmingham, my bedroom became the guest room, and I gladly gave it up for him. He loved the lunches I prepared for him—usually tomato soup and grilled cheese sandwiches. He would compliment me as though I had prepared a gourmet meal.

My grandfather was an amazing man. He believed in giving his children and grandchildren names that meant something, like parents did in biblical times.

"Names have a purpose," he explained. He told me that every time a person says my name, he or she is recalling the attributes of my name into my very lifeblood.

I later found out that *Carolyn* also means "little champion." My schoolteachers and some family members referred to me as "stubborn." But I like "little champion" (or perhaps "determined") much better.

I didn't understand the full meaning of my grandfather's

statement about the power of names until I grew up. And in remembering his words, I saw another aspect of who my grandfather was—a person who used every means possible to bring something positive and admirable into the life of a little girl of color who lived in the heart of racially segregated Birmingham. True to his occupation, he created teaching moments in everything he did.

⊕

Several years earlier, my "strong one" name had been severely challenged. It was August 1957, and I was nine years old. For the first time in my young life, I didn't feel very strong. My grandfather pulled his car into our family's front yard and honked the horn. Mama and I and the rest of the children ran outside. I peeked in the car's backseat and saw my grandmother, Mama Lessie. Grandfather had placed her head on a bed pillow and wrapped her frail body in blankets. In the August heat, she lay very still, and I saw pain written across her face.

"I think it's time we took Lessie to the hospital," Grandfather whispered to my mother. "She's been hurting and bleeding for a while now. I fear something bad is wrong with her."

Grandfather and Daddy lifted Mama Lessie in their muscular arms, took her inside the house, and laid her on Mama's bed. Not long after, Mama told them she felt we needed to call an ambulance. The ambulance took my grandmother to nearby Princeton Hospital, and we followed by car. I expected the nurses to put her in a clean room in the main hospital ward, where doctors could treat her and make her well.

They didn't. They took Mama Lessie down the back stairs into the bowels of Princeton Hospital and placed her on a small bed. Other people of color lay down there, too, moaning and groaning in unrelieved pain.

"Why are they putting Mama Lessie in the basement?" I asked Mama.

"Never mind, Carolyn," she said. "Just help us get her settled."

I looked around the basement where my beloved grandmother lay on her back, still and quiet. It was a small, closed-in space, with sweating water pipes climbing across the walls and ceiling. Big drops of water fell onto the cold, brick-and-cobblestone floor.

"Carolyn, you'll be staying here with Mama Lessie and taking care of her while I'm at work. After I get off, I'll bring her supper, and you can go home and rest. But she needs someone to stay with her all the time down here, and since you are the girl-child . . . well, it'll be your job."

"Will we have to stay down here in the basement?" I asked.

"Yes, Carolyn, and I'll depend on you to take care of her while she's here in the hospital."

It was a tremendous responsibility for a nine-year-old. I felt like a big girl, and I was proud I'd been asked to help. But I also felt afraid. I loved my grandmother. I wondered what the future held for her. And for me.

My hope for my grandmother's recovery faded day by day

as I sat in the basement of Princeton Hospital and watched her suffer. I sang the song I had heard so many times before at my grandfather's church. The words always gave me strength and courage:

All along this Christian journey,
I want Jesus to walk with me.
I want Jesus to walk with me.
All along this Christian journey,
I want Jesus to walk with me.
In my troubles, walk with me.
When I'm dying, walk with me.
All along this Christian journey,
I want Jesus to walk with me.
I want Jesus to walk with me.

I had never seen Mama Lessie like this. She was only fifty-four years old, but she looked much older. To pass the hours, I counted the beads of water as they dropped from the pipes. Then I counted the redbrick squares on the floor and thought about my life with Mama Lessie and all the wonderful things I'd done with her and learned from her. I didn't want any of that to end.

⊕

Born in Columbiana, Alabama, my grandmother had a gentle nature and soft-spoken ways. She never yelled at me—not once. She never punished me either. When I needed correction, she instructed me in a gentle and loving way, always teaching me lessons about life and love and God as she disciplined me. Mama Lessie was a good writer and organizer. She had the ability to sound out words and then write them down correctly. I have been told by family members that I inherited my gift of spelling from my grandmother.

My grandmother had told me I was precocious. I had no idea what that meant, but she said it with a smile on her lips and a twinkle in her eye. I spent most of the summers at my grandparents' house while my mother took classes. Together each summer, Mama Lessie and I worked at the vacation Bible schools in Granddaddy's two churches, as well as other churches that had only occasional guest pastors and no full-time pastors. We taught the children how to make pot holders out of yarn and how to glue rice, glitter, and tinsel to paper plates to make collages for their folks. We also created the final programs, held after each session.

When all the vacation Bible schools ended, I would watch Mama Lessie sew at her old sewing machine. She made clothes for her five daughters throughout their lifetimes, and she also made curtains for the windows and sewed quilts for the beds. Afternoons with my grandmother meant picking greens, cabbage, okra, and tomatoes in the small garden my grandfather planted in the backyard each spring.

"Why do you and Grandfather always eat so much cabbage and okra?" I asked her once.

Mama Lessie smiled. "It's because we both wear dentures, Carolyn, and we raise and cook the things we can eat."

Oftentimes, Granddaddy came home from work, put us grandchildren in the backseat of his car, and took us to pick wild strawberries and blackberries along the roadside. We'd take the berries back to Mama Lessie and eat them as fast as she could wash them.

Sometimes my grandfather took us into downtown Clanton. He had befriended just about everybody in that city, both black and white. He was the person folks called for advice, prayer, and practical help when someone got into trouble or ended up in jail. He was the one people went to when a baby was born or when someone in the community died or when a couple wanted to get married or when someone needed food or money. At that time in the South, black preachers represented God's own voice and guidance. My grandfather was respected for two reasons: he was a preacher, and he had a college degree.

"Come meet my grandbabies!" he would call out with pride to Clanton's barber or grocer or dry cleaner. Then he would call out our names, one by one, and introduce us to his many friends.

I especially liked those summers in Clanton when it was just Mama Lessie and me. She would walk me across the street to Miss Daisy's beauty shop and sit me in the small room built onto the side of Miss Daisy's house. Then she would stay beside me while Miss Daisy washed and pressed my hair and put real curls in it. Like my father, my grandparents never let me walk anywhere alone. Not even across the street to Miss Daisy's.

"Things can happen to little black girls," my grandfather once told me. I later learned that those "things" meant rape. This was one of the reasons he and my grandmother wouldn't even let me walk across the street alone from their house to get my hair done. Mama Lessie told me there had been incidents of young black girls walking to the store or to a relative's house who were picked up by a carful of white men, raped, and then abandoned. It was commonplace in the South—the greatest fear all black parents had for their girls. Most of these rapes were reported but went unpunished. My granddaddy wanted to protect me, to keep me safe.

"You're our special granddaughter," Mama Lessie often told me while Miss Daisy curled my hair. My grandmother made me feel so loved. At my home in Birmingham, I just felt like one of six kids. But at Mama Lessie's, I was special—an individual, precious, *girl*-grand-*child*. She had, after all, raised five very special daughters of her own.

⊕

In the basement of Princeton Hospital during those long two weeks, I stayed by Mama Lessie's side. Various doctors came down infrequently, pulling a small white partition around the bed to offer my grandmother some limited privacy. They checked her heart and took her blood pressure but didn't do much to treat her actual illness. And no doctor ever spoke to the frightened little black girl who trembled in the chair beside the dying woman. I felt invisible.

Hired hospital help brought in food trays on a pretty regular schedule, but Mama Lessie never ate a bite. I kept looking into her face as I sat beside her, hoping she would talk to me. But she never said a single word during those weeks at Princeton Hospital. Not one word.

With each passing day, my fears grew, until they were as tall as the old apple tree my grandfather had planted long ago behind the garage at his Clanton home—the tree his children and grandchildren climbed to pick green apples. I was confused. No one told me why Mama Lessie had gotten sick or if she would ever recover and come home. During those dark days my name should have been "the timid one" or "the scared one," not Carolyn, "the strong one."

Mama Lessie became weaker and frailer with each passing day. At times I closed my eyes and fought hard to remember my two favorite photos of her—her wedding picture and her graduation picture.

⊕

My grandfather had married Lessie Lane sometime around her sixteenth birthday. In the lone, faded, wedding photograph, she is looking directly into the camera, her eyes serious and somber, her small body robed in a full-sleeved, polka-dot wedding dress. Her soft, dark hair is smoothed stylishly around her youthful face, with a slight puff of hair combed

FROM MARTIN LUTHER KING JR.'S "I HAVE A DREAM" SPEECH

I say to you today, my friends, that in spite of the difficulties and frustrations of the moment, I still have a dream. It is a dream deeply rooted in the American dream.

I have a dream that one day this nation will rise up and live out the true meaning of its creed: "We hold these truths to be self-evident: that all men are created equal."

I have a dream that one day on the red hills of Georgia the sons of former slaves and the sons of former slaveowners will be able to sit down together at a table of brotherhood.

I have a dream that one day even the state of Mississippi, a desert state, sweltering with the heat of injustice and oppression, will be transformed into an oasis of freedom and justice.

I have a dream that my four children will one day live in a nation where they will not be judged by the color of their skin but by the content of their character.

I have a dream today.

I have a dream that one day the state of Alabama, whose governor's lips are presently dripping with the words of interposition and nullification, will be transformed into a situation where little black boys and black girls will be able to join hands with little white boys and white girls and walk together as sisters and brothers.

I have a dream today.

I have a dream that one day every valley shall be exalted, every hill and mountain shall be made low, the rough places will be made plain, and the crooked places will be made straight, and the glory of the Lord shall be revealed, and all flesh shall see it together.

This is our hope. This is the faith with which I return to the South. With this faith we will be able to hew out of the mountain of despair a stone of hope. With this faith we will be able to transform the jangling discords of our nation into a beautiful symphony of brotherhood. With this faith we will be able to work together, to pray together, to struggle together, to go to jail together, to stand up for freedom together, knowing that we will be free one day.

This will be the day when all of God's children will be able to sing with a new meaning, "My country, 'tis of thee, sweet land of liberty, of thee I sing. Land where my fathers died, land of the pilgrim's pride, from every mountainside, let freedom ring."

And if America is to be a great nation this must become true. So let freedom ring from the prodigious hilltops of New Hampshire. Let freedom ring from the mighty mountains of New York. Let freedom ring from the heightening Alleghenies of Pennsylvania!

Let freedom ring from the snowcapped Rockies of Colorado!

Let freedom ring from the curvaceous peaks of California!

But not only that; let freedom ring from Stone Mountain of Georgia!

Let freedom ring from Lookout Mountain of Tennessee!

Let freedom ring from every hill and every molehill of Mississippi. From every mountainside, let freedom ring.

When we let freedom ring, when we let it ring from every village and every hamlet, from every state and every city, we will be able to speed up that day when all of God's children, black men and white men, Jews and Gentiles, Protestants and Catholics, will be able to join hands and sing in the words of the old Negro spiritual, "Free at last! free at last! Thank God Almighty, we are free at last!"[1]

just so to rise from the top of her head. A large round medallion hangs from her neck. In her hands she holds an assortment of wildflowers—nothing fancy. Perhaps she stopped the buggy and picked them from a roadside field on the way to her wedding.

During those early years of marriage, she birthed five daughters for her hardworking husband. After the girls were born and Mama Lessie passed age thirty, she was able to fulfill her long-held dream: to go back to school. Granddaddy had graduated from the high school of Selma University in 1920. From there he attended Alabama State Teachers College in Montgomery and earned his bachelor of science degree. Selma University later honored him with a doctor of divinity degree. He wanted his wife to have the same educational privileges he had had.

Several years later someone snapped Mama Lessie's photograph in her black graduation cap and gown. In that photo she wears a slight smile and a combined expression of hope and accomplishment. I am certain she was thinking of the future for her daughters and unborn granddaughters on that day of tremendous accomplishment. Sure enough, all five of her daughters graduated from college. Three became teachers, one became a nurse, and one became a dietitian.

⊕

Now, laid up in the basement of Princeton Hospital, Mama Lessie's expression held neither hope nor accomplishment.

Each evening as I waited for Mama to bring my grandmother's home-cooked supper and to relieve me, I sat quietly and watched Mama Lessie slowly die.

Mama Lessie passed away one night in late August 1957, on Mama's watch. In later years we learned that her symptoms (severe vaginal bleeding and stabbing gut pain) probably indicated female cancer.

On Saturday morning August 31, 1957, in the cemetery at Union Baptist Church, we laid Mama Lessie—Mrs. Lessie V. Burt—to rest.

⊕

The worship service was about to begin at Sixteenth Street Baptist Church on Sunday morning, September 15, 1963. The clock was ticking. I knew I had only a few minutes left to collect the rest of the reports and write the Sunday school summary. I was looking forward to Reverend Cross's sermon that morning. He had posted the title on the board outside the church: "A Love That Forgives." The sermon was to be based on Luke 23:34, the words Christ spoke from the cross: "Father, forgive them, for they do not know what they are doing."

As I quickly made my way into the sanctuary, I glanced at the large antique clock that hung on the church wall. The time was 10:22 a.m.

CHAPTER 4

THE BOMB HEARD 'ROUND THE WORLD

Sunday morning, September 15, 1963

⊕

I'm concerned about a better world. I'm concerned about justice;
I'm concerned about brotherhood; I'm concerned about truth. And
when one is concerned about that, he can never advocate violence.
For through violence you may murder a murderer, but you can't
murder murder. Through violence you may murder a liar, but you
can't establish truth. Through violence you may murder a hater,
but you can't murder hate through violence. Darkness cannot put
out darkness; only light can do that.

MARTIN LUTHER KING JR.,
"Where Do We Go from Here?" [1]

I WALKED INTO THE SANCTUARY, toward the stained-glass window of Jesus, his kind face and loving eyes focused on me, and that's when I heard it. *Boom!* The blast shook the building.

Thunder? I thought. *Maybe a lightning strike?*

The sound was muffled, not loud and earth shattering like the bombs I had heard so many times when Klan members dynamited black homes and businesses throughout the city.

Glass cracked and crashed to the floor, but I barely noticed. I just wanted to get out of there.

What is happening? I asked myself.

Someone shouted, "Hit the floor!"

I dropped. Sprawled out flat in the aisle on the sanctuary floor, I still held the Sunday school reports in my hands.

Seconds passed—one . . . two . . . three . . . four . . . five. I heard no more sounds. No breaking glass. No movement. No voices. Just silence. Dead silence. More seconds passed— six . . . seven . . . eight . . . nine. Fear enveloped me. *What is happening!* For at least ten full seconds, no one moved. Nothing happened.

Then I heard and felt on the floor beneath me a stampede of feet—moving, running, scurrying to escape the building. Jumping up from the floor, I ran to the nearby exit and looked outside.

What is going on? Police cars were everywhere.

How could they get here so quickly? The church was already surrounded, and police were putting up barricades on the streets around the building.

Chaos ruled. Several church members stood outside with stunned expressions. Heads were cut and bleeding. Loved ones wiped their blood-wet faces. Mrs. Demand ran outside, her lower leg gashed by flying glass and her shoe filled with blood. Parents were frantically searching for their children.

Now I knew for sure it was a bomb. I ran out the door looking for my two brothers. *How could there be a bomb here? in my church?* I could hardly comprehend such a thought. I had heard bombs go off in my neighborhood, but it seemed unfathomable that it could happen in this safe haven.

I looked up at the stained-glass Jesus window that stood above me and searched for the face that had always brought me such comfort, security, and peace. The window was intact, its glass unbroken . . . except . . . except for the face of Jesus. The bomb had cleanly blown away his face. Nothing else. Just his face.

⊕

Outside the building, a large number of black folks were angry. People from the neighborhood and the nearby boardinghouse had heard the commotion and were now pouring onto the church property. They were ready to fight.

"You bombed our church!" they screamed to no one in particular. "You hurt our people!"

They struggled to get through the police-enforced boundaries. They didn't know exactly who had set the dynamite, but they were desperate to get even, to strike out at someone—anyone.

As black residents paced outside the church, they ranted and threatened. "We can't let this pass!"

But no fights broke out. Police kept tight control on the people, on the ugly chaos. Pastor John Cross walked through the crowd with a megaphone, tears streaming down his face, and begged the crowd to be calm and nonviolent. "The Lord is our Shepherd," the pastor called out. "We shall not want!"

Just then a thought hit me like a baseball bat. *My brothers! Where are my brothers?*

I wanted to get out of there as fast as I could and run straight home.

But where are Wendell and Kirk? They are my responsibility. I can't go home without them.

Shouting their names, I dashed back into the building and began to search for them. Rubble and broken glass littered the floor, but I barely noticed. I was thinking only, *Where are those boys?* I paused at the women's restroom door but did not venture inside. It wasn't even recognizable as a restroom anymore—there was just a gaping hole piled up with dirt and bricks.

No, they wouldn't be in here. They hate girls!

Maybe they're still in their Sunday school room, where I dropped them off this morning. Or maybe they are hiding in the men's bathroom.

I checked both rooms. No boys.

They could be outside by now!

I stepped outside into the confusion and racket. I felt panicky. My brothers seemed to have disappeared.

Okay, one more time—the women's restroom. That might have been the only place the boys could find shelter.

As I leaned into the restroom doorway, all I could see was a huge pile of rubble, almost four feet high, in the middle of the tile floor. Ash. Dirt. Soot. And silence. No sound came from the rubble or from anywhere else in the room. *No one's in here*, I thought as I turned around and ran back outside.

In the midst of the confusion, I saw carloads of white people circling the church and then driving off with screeching tires. They were laughing and singing a little song: "Two, four, six, eight! We don't want to integrate!" I was frightened. My parents never preached hatred to us children. I could not understand this action—the height of evil.

To my relief, I saw my father across the street. He was behind a huge barricade, arguing with a police officer. He looked frantic. "Let me through!" he shouted to the officer. "I've got two children in there!" I was so glad to see him— that meant I could finally go home. I still didn't know at that point if anyone had been hurt, but I believed my dad would help me find my brothers.

Two children? No, Daddy, three!

Somehow my father managed to push through the barricade. I ran into his arms and screamed, "Daddy! I don't know where Wendell and Kirk are. I've looked everywhere. I can't find them!"

"It's okay, Carolyn," my father shouted back above the racket. "Wendell's in the car. He's safe."

"But what about Kirk?" I cried.

"I'm sure some of the church members took Kirk home with them."

My father drove us home. When we turned into the driveway, we saw Mama standing anxiously at the front door.

"A man just called," she told us. "He said, 'I've got this little fella here with me. He won't turn me loose. He says his name is Kirk. I found your number in the phone book under "Maull." If you can come get him, I'll keep him right with me until you get here.'"

My parents jumped in the car and hurried to find Kirk.

I later found out that after the bomb exploded, Kirk took off running outside. My brother grabbed the leg of the first person he saw—a man walking down the street—and held on tight. He absolutely refused to let go. Somehow the man got Kirk's last name out of him. Since only three Maulls were listed in the phone book, he found our number and called us.

Kirk became a quiet child after that September morning. He seemingly lost his desire for conversation. All his teachers told my parents, "Kirk's such a smart child, but he never talks." I believe the bombing somehow damaged my little brother. He was never quite the same.

My brother Wendell took off running when the bomb exploded, too, and headed toward downtown. Driving back to the church from his weekend job, my father saw Wendell standing in the street. He stopped the car, hugged him tightly, and put the terrified boy in the car.

⊕

By noon that day, Mama and Daddy, Chester, Wendell, Kirk, Agnes, and I were sitting at home. Silent. Stunned. No one said anything. We knew a bomb had exploded in our church, but we didn't know why. In our own lonely silence, each of us tried to make some sense of it.

That afternoon, around one o'clock, Carole's mother, Mrs. Alpha Robertson, phoned Mama.

"Is your Carolyn at home?" she asked.

"Yes, Alpha," Mama told her. "Carolyn is here with me."

"Well," she said, "if your Carolyn is home, maybe my Carole went home with somebody from church."

That afternoon my family and I all stayed around the house, not talking about much of anything. No one mentioned the Cavalettes' meeting, but there was an unspoken understanding that we wouldn't meet that day. Everything just seemed to freeze in time.

Around four o'clock that afternoon the telephone again interrupted our silence. Mama answered, then told us the news she had just received.

"There were four girls in the restroom who never made it out," she said. "They're all dead." She touched me on the shoulder as she told me this news. Mama didn't cry, but she seemed very sad—a soft kind of sadness. She didn't say it, but I imagine she was grateful I was still alive—that all three of her children who were at church were alive. And I'm sure she was also thanking God for bringing her children home safely.

My mind was whirling. *In the restroom? No, it can't be. I was just in there. I didn't see anyone. And I didn't hear anything.*

"They found them buried under a pile of rubble," Mama said.

"Who were they, Mama?" I asked.

"Addie, Denise, Carole, and Cynthia."

No! No! No! It can't be! I'd spoken to them seconds before the bomb exploded. I'd stood right there and talked with them.

"Some woman claims she saw Tommy Blanton's Chevrolet parked a block from the church around two o'clock this morning. Said she saw three white men in the car, and one of them was 'Dynamite Bob' Chambliss."

Little did I know that the loss of those girls was, ironically, the real beginning of hope for blacks and whites in Birmingham. Their blood—the "blood of the innocents"— had spilled on the hands of Birmingham's people. And now, finally, the whole world was watching.

CHAPTER 5

LIFE IS BUT A VAPOR

✠

Why, you do not even know what will happen tomorrow. What is your life? You are a mist that appears for a little while and then vanishes.

JAMES 4:14

Four or more who were attending Sunday School at Sixteenth Street Baptist Church on the day of Sorrow and Shame were killed. Their bodies were stacked up on top of each other like bales of hay from the crumbling ruins left by the dynamiting. They were girls. They were children. . . . Those who died in the September 15 bombing also died serving the Lord Jesus Christ, who was crucified. This will be an unforgettable day in our nation, in world history, in the new rebellion of which the Confederate flags seem to symbolize. Yet, if members of the Negro group pour into the churches on Sunday, stream to the voter-registration offices, make their dollars talk freedom, and build up a better leadership, those children might not have died in vain.

"KILLERS OF THE INNOCENTS—COMMENTARY,"
Birmingham World, September 18, 1963

WHEN THE WORDS CAME OUT of Mama's mouth, I think my heart stopped beating. I could barely breathe. My whole body went suddenly numb.

"Addie? Denise? Carole? And *Cynthia*?" I asked.

Mama nodded.

"My best friend, Cynthia? Dead? Are you sure, Mama?"

Mama just nodded her head.

Images of Cynthia raced through my mind. We had planned to meet that very afternoon with the Cavalettes club members. This was the day we were going to pay for our matching caps and T-shirts.

Does this mean I won't ever see her again or talk with her on the phone?

The girls are gone, dead. I repeated the words over and over in my mind, as if trying to convince myself. *The girls are gone, dead.*

Mentally I retraced my steps from that morning. With a jolt, I remembered the phone call. "Three minutes," the male caller had said. In the aftermath, we learned that the bomb had blown a seven-foot-high, three-foot-deep hole in the restroom wall. It had also demolished the stairs—the steps I had climbed only seconds before the blast.

I struggled to let the awful news sink in. *My friends were lying dead under all that mess of rubble? They were there, under the debris in the bathroom?*

Don't think about it, Carolyn, an inner voice warned.

But if I had stayed in the bathroom one minute longer to talk . . .

Put it out of your mind, Carolyn, the voice urged.

Or if I had left my own Sunday school class just two minutes later . . . I sucked in a breath. *I would have died in the bathroom with those girls.*

My brush with death had been close. Terrifyingly close. The realization was too painful to mention out loud, and almost unbearable to think about.

I am alive and safe at home. But they are gone, dead.

⊕

It was several months before I found out that Sarah Collins, Addie's sister, had also been in that restroom. Sarah later related to me her account of what happened that morning. "I couldn't see anything," she said. The flying glass had penetrated Sarah's eyes. She ended up being hospitalized for two months, losing one eye completely and retaining only partial vision in the other. She would never be the same again.

A few moments after the blast, Sarah had called out for her sister: "Addie! Addie! Addie?" When she heard no response, she called out again, louder this time. "Addie!" Sarah imagined the other girls had run off and left her. She didn't know they lay just a few feet from her . . . dead beneath the rubble.

Mr. Rutledge, a deacon in our church, heard Sarah's cries and moans. He followed the sound of her voice and rushed into the restroom. He found Sarah entombed in debris, about five feet from the rest of the girls' bodies. He lifted her up and carried her to a waiting ambulance outside. In the hospital that day, there was one glimmer of hope in the midst of so much tragedy: a little black girl with pieces of glass penetrating her face did not have to experience the same treatment my grandmother had just a few years earlier. Thanks to the courage of a white nurse named Jim Jones, the whites-only University Hospital admitted Addie, purposely and intentionally breaking segregation rules.

Two more deacons ran inside the restroom. They dug through the rubble with their bare hands. Other church members, however, stayed a good distance back. They were afraid to go into the restroom, assuming the Klan had prepared a second charge of dynamite and more deadly bombs would follow the first explosion after a crowd had formed.

While the deacons clawed at the pile of broken glass and bricks, Reverend prayed aloud that another bomb had not been planted and that God would keep them safe.

Soon someone saw a hand sticking out from the debris. They kept digging until they uncovered each girl. The girls lay lifeless on top of each other in a pile that resembled stacked-up firewood. One by one their bodies were lifted from the rubble.

From what I heard later, the blast had rendered the girls' bodies unrecognizable. Cynthia's head was dismembered from the rest of her body. Her family identified her by the birthstone ring found on her finger.

A large, sharp stone had embedded itself in Denise's skull during the explosion. At the morgue, Denise's mother removed the rock and took it home with her. She placed it in a glass case and kept it for years in the family's photography studio.

Shortly after the bombing, the FBI summoned my friend Junie Collins to accompany them. Her parents weren't home when the agents came, and since Junie was the oldest child in the family, it fell to her to assume adult-level responsibility. She thought she was going to see her sister, Addie, in the hospital. Instead, they took her to the morgue to identify Addie's body. Junie later told me, "If my life depended on it, I couldn't say *this* was my sister. But then I saw this little brown shoe—like a loafer—on her foot. And I knew it was Addie."

I did not see the bodies, but in the coming days I read the paralyzing and chilling descriptions in the newspaper. I shook my head and covered my eyes, attempting to remove the horrible images from my mind. I didn't want to know the gruesome details. But it was too late—over the long years since the bombing, the painful images have continued to recall themselves to me.

⊕

My family and I were in shock. Complete disbelief. Over the course of the evening—through phone calls, the radio, and the evening news—we pieced together what had happened that morning. The story surfaced in bits and pieces, like segments of a strange puzzle.

We sat at home in stunned silence.

Someone had turned on the television. We turned it off because we couldn't continue to watch the news. I felt more frightened than ever. An air of woe and doom came over me. A voice inside my head kept telling me, *They missed you this time, Carolyn. But the girls are dead. You were there— you talked with them right before they died.*

At that moment, the bombings in Birmingham took on a new twist for me. People were dead. And these were people I knew! The racial situation had now become very real and very personal.

My young, innocent mind made another powerful note: It happened in my church! Church had always been a special place, a haven where we worshiped God. It was *his* place— a spot reserved each week just for God.

My parents had drilled into our brains the sacredness of God's house. "In church, we don't run," they explained with definite seriousness in their voices. "We don't chew gum. We don't eat food. We don't talk loud. We don't play. Church is a place where we show respect and reverence."

Instead we had people planting bombs in our church and my friends dying there.

Until that moment, I had not understood the depth of the volatility between blacks and whites in Birmingham. I could not fathom the extent of the hatred some whites had for black people.

Oh, I knew about segregation, about the protests and marches down city streets, about black people trying to get the "whites only" and "coloreds" signs taken down from restroom doors, restaurants, train stations, and city buses. But I had always felt protected by my father, my grandfather, my brothers, and my church. Before September 15, 1963, I didn't know to worry about dying because of my skin color. But the thought kept echoing and refused to leave my mind: *People will actually kill us over this! What is this thing about skin?*

And I felt helpless because I was just a child and I couldn't change anything.

⊕

That Sunday evening Dr. Martin Luther King Jr. wired President Kennedy from Atlanta, telling him he was going to Birmingham to plead with blacks to remain nonviolent. He added that unless "immediate Federal steps are taken," there will be "in Birmingham and Alabama the worst racial holocaust this Nation has ever seen."[1] President Kennedy was yachting off Newport, Rhode Island, and was notified of the bombing by radiotelephone. Attorney General Robert F. Kennedy ordered his chief Civil Rights troubleshooter, Burke Marshall, to Birmingham, along with twenty-five FBI agents and bomb experts from Washington, D.C.[2]

Dr. King also wired Governor George Wallace: "The blood of four little children . . . is on your hands," he wrote. "Your irresponsible and misguided actions have created in Birmingham and Alabama the atmosphere that has induced continued violence and now murder."[3]

Twelve days later, on September 27, *Time* magazine placed on its front cover the steel-cold, angry face of Governor George Wallace with the inscription "Alabama: Civil Rights Battlefield." In the background, the editors placed the photograph of the church's stained-glass window with the kind face of Jesus blown clean away.

⊕

Before darkness fell on the night of September 15, the reverend and his deacons closed the front doors of the wonderful old Sixteenth Street Baptist Church. For the following eight months, the congregation met to worship in the nearby L. R. Hall Auditorium. Money and donations poured into the church from all over the world. Local contractor L. S. Gaillard worked hard to make the needed repairs to the church. He did everything he could to make it a sturdy building—a safe place for young black girls in white Sunday dresses to once again worship God.

Jesus' stained-glass face was also remade and set back in the window. I have no idea why only Christ's face was blown away in the explosion—I have to wonder if perhaps that's just the way God allowed it to happen. Now, thanks to careful restoration, Jesus again looks down upon his congregation with kind, loving eyes.

But as a remembrance of that morning, the reverend and his deacons decided to leave two damaged things in the church untouched and unrepaired. One was the antique clock on the sanctuary wall. In the midst of the bombing, the old timepiece stayed attached to the wall, its glass case intact and undisturbed. But for some reason its faithful tick and accurate hands stopped dead at the exact moment of the blast—10:22.

Nearly five decades later, the clock—in unmoving silence—tells the story to worshipers and to pilgrims who walk through the church doors.

The girls' restroom—the place where the bomb exploded—has also remained frozen in time. After the bombing it was simply sealed up. A wall was built in front of the restroom door as if to say, "Forget that it happened!"

But some of us refuse to forget. We will forever worship on sacred and holy ground.

⊕

Slipping into bed that night, I felt sick. I was afraid to close my eyes. So I started to sing:

All along this Christian journey,
I want Jesus to walk with me.
I want Jesus to walk with me.
All along this Christian journey,
I want Jesus to walk with me.
In my troubles, walk with me.
When I'm dying, walk with me.
All along this Christian journey,
I want Jesus to walk with me.
I want Jesus to walk with me.

Is this going to continue? I asked myself late that night as I scooted deeper under the blankets. *Will this wave of killing and bombs ever end?*

The thought of death and bombs frightened me. I felt powerless to do anything about the hatred and violence in this city—my city.

My inner voice spoke loud and clear to me: *Carolyn, it's not* if *you will get blown up and killed by a bomb, but* when. *It's just a matter of time, and then it will be your turn. One day a bomb will explode, and you will not escape it. Like Denise, Addie, Carole, and Cynthia.*

I finally drifted off into a troubled, restless sleep. Darkness engulfed Birmingham, Alabama, on that tragic day of sorrow and shame. And a heavy, incomprehensible dark cloud of depression and sadness settled over my own head and heart—a nightmarish web of memories that would hover over me for many years to come.

The following week I went to Fred Singleton's sporting-goods store. With my saved-up money, I bought Cynthia's gold cap and shirt. Her name, "Cynthia," was printed in black letters on the front of the shirt, and the letter *C*, for Cavalettes, was printed on the back. I gave the cap and shirt to Cynthia's mother, Mrs. Wesley. I realize now it was a small token, but it was my way of saying how important Cynthia was to me—to all of us. Almost five decades later, I still have my gold cap. It hurts me to look at it.

⊕

We had had unsolved bombings for years in my city. Bombs exploded, and the city of Birmingham went on with business as usual. No arrests were made, so there were no convictions. We heard no public apologies, few empathetic speeches from the white community. No one sent letters of righteous indignation or sympathy. A bomb exploded, and it proved just another day in the life of Birmingham Negroes.

We knew that on any day, at any time, a bomb might explode. After a blast the phone would ring, and the caller would tell us the bomb's location. Our family would spend the rest of the evening quiet and somber, often in prayer, contemplating such a depth of hatred and depravity. Black people somehow adapted to the blasts—the destroyed homes, businesses, and churches. It was our way of life, a cross that each of us thought we had to bear.

Lord, can we really bear this cross?

It was one thing to turn our heads when a building had been smashed. But now four girls had died.

This event proved a pivotal point in my life and in my church, and in the nation as well.

On the day after the church bombing, a young, white Birmingham attorney, Charles Morgan Jr., publicly blamed the pillars of the city for the girls' deaths. "Every person in this community who has in any way contributed during the past several years to the popularity of hatred is at least as guilty, or more so, than the demented fool who threw that bomb," Mr. Morgan said.

He blamed politicians who catered to racist votes, newspaper editors who fueled the racial tension, and church and business leaders who refused to take responsibility for the pervasive racial hatred in the city. "We all did it," he said. "Every one of us is condemned for that crime and the bombing before it and for the one last month, last year, a decade ago. We all did it."

Then he added, "Birmingham is not a dying city; it is dead."

The speech destroyed his budding law practice, led to death threats against his family, and got him run out of town.[4]

⊕

Scripture tells us that life is but a vapor (see James 4:14, NKJV). The morning of the bombing my friends and I had looked forward to a Sunday afternoon Cavalettes club meeting. Just that morning I had spoken with them face-to-face. But now they were gone. With a sudden explosion, like an invisible breath or vapor, four young girls simply vanished. I was overwhelmed with disbelief. This feeling would last a long time. I tried hard to process what happened at church on my own, attempting to put everything together, to make sense of it all. But it would get worse for me before it got better.

CHAPTER 6

FOUR LITTLE COFFINS

⊕

The innocent blood of these little girls may well serve as a redemptive force that will bring new light to this dark city.

DR. MARTIN LUTHER KING JR.

And so this afternoon in a real sense [the four girls who died] have something to say to each of us in their death. They have something to say to every minister of the gospel who has remained silent behind the safe security of stained-glass windows. They have something to say to every politician who has fed his constituents with the stale bread of hatred and the spoiled meat of racism. They have something to say to a federal government that has compromised with the undemocratic practices of southern Dixiecrats and the blatant hypocrisy of right-wing northern Republicans. They have something to say to every Negro who has passively accepted the evil system of segregation and who has stood on the sidelines in a mighty struggle for justice. They say to each of us, black and white alike, that we must substitute courage for caution. They say to us that we must be concerned not merely about who murdered them, but about the system, the way of life, the philosophy which produced the murderers. Their death says to us that we must work passionately and unrelentingly for the realization of the American dream.

DR. MARTIN LUTHER KING JR.,
funeral service for Addie Mae Collins, Denise McNair, and Cynthia Diane Wesley[1]

THE MURDERED GIRLS' FAMILIES began making funeral preparations for their young daughters first thing that Monday morning. Sixteenth Street Baptist Church gave each dead girl's family some funds to bury their daughter.

Carole's family held her funeral on Tuesday, September 17, 1963, at St. John AME Church, separate from the service for the other girls. By the time Carole's mother found out about the joint service, she had already made the funeral arrangements for Carole. She also felt this was personal— she had lost her daughter, and she wanted to grieve in a less public way.

The next day, Wednesday, Dr. Martin Luther King Jr. delivered the eulogy for Addie, Denise, and Cynthia at a joint funeral. The service was held at nearby Sixth Avenue Baptist Church, since our church was closed for repairs. More than eight thousand mourners, including eight hundred clergy of both races, attended the service. The old church seated only about a thousand people, so most of the crowd stood outside, facing the front door. No city officials, however, braved the crowds to come.

I didn't attend the funerals either. I just couldn't face the row of small coffins. It was sometime later that I heard Dr. King's speech:

> This afternoon, we gather in the quiet of this
> sanctuary to pay our last tribute of respect to these
> beautiful children of God. They entered the stage
> of history just a few years ago, and in the brief years

that they were privileged to act on this mortal stage, they played their parts exceedingly well. Now the curtain falls; they move through the exit; the drama of their earthly life comes to a close. They are now committed back to that eternity from which they came. These children—unoffending, innocent, and beautiful—were the victims of one of the most vicious and tragic crimes ever perpetrated against humanity. And yet they died nobly. They are the martyred heroines of a holy crusade for freedom and human dignity.[2]

The media didn't cover others whose lives were irrevocably altered that day. Sarah Collins, Addie's sister who survived the restroom blast, ended up losing her right eye and retained just 30 percent of the vision in her left eye. After two months in the hospital, she came home with a glass eye inserted in her right eye socket. She called it her "drugstore eye." Drugstore eyes (like cosmetics in those days) were made for white people, not black people. The glass eyes came in shades of green, blue, and light brown, not dark brown or black for African-Americans. Sarah's family, with seven children, had little money to buy Sarah a custom-made eye.

Little Sarah made an incredible journey throughout life with mismatched eyes—one of the many challenges she would face in the years ahead. But none of her injuries compared with the wounds to her spirit. The only living witness to what happened in the restroom at 10:22 a.m. on

September 15, 1963, Sarah chose to live in silence and seclusion for many years.

Dr. King's funeral message served as a sobering call for justice. But woven throughout was his trademark ray of hope:

> And so my friends, they did not die in vain. God still has a way of wringing good out of evil. And history has proven over and over again that unmerited suffering is redemptive. The innocent blood of these little girls may well serve as a redemptive force that will bring new light to this dark city. The holy Scripture says, "A little child shall lead them." The death of these little children may lead our whole Southland from the low road of man's inhumanity to man to the high road of peace and brotherhood. These tragic deaths may lead our nation to substitute an aristocracy of character for an aristocracy of color. The spilled blood of these innocent girls may cause the whole citizenry of Birmingham to transform the negative extremes of a dark past into the positive extremes of a bright future. Indeed this tragic event may cause the white South to come to terms with its conscience.[3]

Dr. King was right, but that redemptive work wouldn't start happening right away. In the time immediately after the church bombing, no one spoke of the tragedy or the girls who died. Not the afternoon of the bombing. Not that night.

Not the next day or the next month or the next year. After the funerals, no one mentioned again the four dead girls— my friends. Not my parents, not my teachers, not my pastor, not my Sunday school teachers, not my church members, not my friends. No one. It was like the word *cancer*. No one wanted to say it out loud or acknowledge it. And with the restroom "death chamber" sealed off and walled up, offering no visible reminder of the bombing, it was almost as if it never happened.

CHAPTER 7

THE AFTERMATH

✦

The wanton, brutal crime [the church bombing] sickened Americans on both sides of the Mason-Dixon line and gave new impetus to the drive for civil-rights legislation. As nothing else had done—or perhaps could do—it epitomized the ugliness of racial conflict.

SATURDAY EVENING POST (JUNE 6, 1964)[1]

I stand here to say this afternoon to all assembled here, that in spite of the darkness of this hour, we must not despair. We must not become bitter, nor must we harbor the desire to retaliate with violence. No, we must not lose faith in our white brothers. Somehow we must believe that the most misguided among them can learn to respect the dignity and the worth of all human personality.

MARTIN LUTHER KING JR.,
funeral service for Addie Mae Collins, Denise McNair,
and Cynthia Diane Wesley[2]

As a little girl, I remember hearing stories about my grandmother, Mama Lessie, sitting at the front window of her home holding a loaded Smith & Wesson. My preacher grandfather traveled a lot in those days. Mama Lessie had five little girls to protect, one of them my mother. During long dark nights, alone with her daughters, she watched at the window, her gun loaded and aimed, until her husband came home. Perhaps she, too, sang,

All along this Christian journey,
I want Jesus to walk with me.
I want Jesus to walk with me.

Mama Lessie told her five daughters never to open the door to a stranger, especially a white man. She cautioned them about their dealings with white people because she had seen firsthand some of the things white men had done to Clanton's black folk. One day her daughter Dorothy, about seven years old at the time, went to answer a knock on their front door. She looked out the door's small window, and without opening the door, she ran back to Mama Lessie.

"Mama!" she cried. "There's some white man at the door!"

Mama Lessie walked to the door and looked out the window. Then she quickly opened the door and invited the man inside.

"Dorothy!" she said and then laughed. "That's your uncle Johnny! He's Daddy's brother!"

Dorothy had never met Uncle Johnny before that day. His straight black hair and white skin scared her.

In later years, when Mama Lessie told me this story, I wondered, *If he was an uncle, why did Johnny have white skin?* Eventually I discovered that my maternal grandfather had a white daddy.

After my friends' deaths, I better understood why Mama Lessie had guarded her young brood so carefully. I didn't feel safe anymore. Violence, bombs, and death permeated our lives in those Civil Rights days in Birmingham.

I have never needed it, but I still have Mama Lessie's old Smith & Wesson.

⊕

The Sixteenth Street Baptist Church bombing opened wide the eyes of the United States to racial injustice. Governor Wallace's hard face and tightly knit brows, plastered on the front of *Time* magazine some twelve days later, covered the nation's coffee tables and city newsstands.

When I saw the photograph, I wondered, *Is this the state of things to come?* I remember thinking that Governor Wallace would always be a permanent fixture holding black people back—a roadblock to the progress my people yearned to achieve. Wallace controlled where Alabama's black people lived, where their children went to school, what public facilities they could and could not visit, and where—or if—they would receive hospital and medical care. *Just how*

FROM MARTIN LUTHER KING JR.'S EULOGY SPEECH AFTER THE SIXTEENTH STREET BAPTIST CHURCH BOMBING

May I . . . say a word to you, the members of the bereaved families? It is almost impossible to say anything that can console you at this difficult hour and remove the deep clouds of disappointment which are floating in your mental skies. But I hope you can find a little consolation from the universality of this experience. Death comes to every individual. There is an amazing democracy about death. It is not aristocracy for some of the people, but a democracy for all of the people. Kings die and beggars die; rich men and poor men die; old people die and young people die. Death comes to the innocent and it comes to the guilty. Death is the irreducible common denominator of all men.

I hope you can find some consolation from Christianity's affirmation that death is not the end. Death is not a period that ends the great sentence of life, but a comma that punctuates it to more lofty significance. Death is not a blind alley that leads the human race into a state of nothingness, but an open door which leads man into life eternal. Let this daring faith, this great invincible surmise, be your sustaining power during these trying days. . . .

And so today, you do not walk alone. You gave to this world wonderful children. They didn't live long lives, but they lived meaningful lives. Their lives were distressingly small in quantity, but glowingly large in quality. And no greater tribute can be paid to you as parents, and no greater epitaph can come to them as children, than where they died and what they were doing when they died. They did not die in the dives and dens of Birmingham, nor did they die discussing and listening to filthy jokes. They died between the sacred walls of the church of God, and they were discussing the eternal meaning of love. This stands out as a beautiful, beautiful thing for all generations. Shakespeare had Horatio to say some beautiful words as he stood over the dead body of Hamlet. And today, as I stand over the remains of these beautiful, darling girls, I paraphrase the words of Shakespeare: Good night, sweet princesses. Good night, those who symbolize a new day. And may the flight of angels take thee to thy eternal rest. God bless you.[4]

much influence will this man have on our black population? I wondered. The segregation here wasn't merely established by cultural habits or choices. It was dictated by Alabama's laws about interaction between whites and blacks. To disregard these laws often meant severe punishment.

Since no whites in Alabama, or the rest of the South for that matter, spoke out about the injustices done to black Americans, I assumed that Wallace represented the thoughts and opinions of all white people. Earlier, I might have thought he reflected just white men, because from what I saw, the South's white women didn't appear as violent or as vocal as the men. White women didn't wear Klan robes or aggressively protest integration like their husbands, fathers, brothers, and sons did. Some white women even seemed compassionate and caring toward little black girls and their families. But in 1957, at age nine, I was stunned to see on television and in the newspapers the hate-filled faces of Arkansas's white women— mostly mothers—angrily protesting the "Little Rock Nine." They were adamant that these black students should be banned from the all-white Little Rock Central High School.

By the time I was a teenager, I felt I had no reason to trust a white person. I thought they were all like Governor Wallace.

After the church bombing, sickened by the tragedy that had sent shock waves across the world, President John F. Kennedy sent five hundred armed soldiers to stabilize the city of Birmingham and calm the racial chaos. An article written exclusively for the *Saturday Evening Post* after the bombing captured the president's reaction this way: "President Kennedy, echoing the national temper, said he felt a 'deep sense of outrage and grief.'"[3] The president also flooded our neighborhood with FBI agents from Washington. They visited black homes throughout Birmingham. They interviewed all the members who had attended church on that tragic Sunday morning, and they wrote down what each person said.

When two white FBI men came to my house, my mother and father sat close to me on the sofa. I answered the questions as best I could. The men asked if I had seen "anything suspicious" or "anything unusual" at church that morning before the bombing.

"No," I told them.

They asked, "Can you tell us in your own words what happened?"

I told them everything I remembered. The men seemed disinterested in my answers. Their attitude was cold and matter-of-fact. I told them about the phone call I had received in the office that morning only seconds before the bomb exploded.

"Three minutes," the man had said to me.

The investigators failed to write that down. I wished later I had asked to read the information they'd jotted on their pads of paper.

They also questioned my two brothers about the bombing.

I felt a certain sense of hope that day as I spoke with the FBI. *These men are going to go find the people responsible for killing my friends*, I thought. I knew capturing the criminals wouldn't bring back my friends, but it certainly would get the murderers off our streets.

When these killers are caught and locked up, I reasoned, *I won't have to worry about them planting another bomb in my church. They can't bomb the church and they can't kill me if they're in prison.*

I felt like an adult when I spoke with the FBI. But I wasn't. I was still a kid, and I was still afraid of dying.

The FBI promised the American people they would find the killers. They would conduct the biggest manhunt since the Dillinger case, they said.

But time passed, and no one in our community heard a word about the case. Whenever we called and asked about the progress being made to catch the bombers, we received the same answer: "The FBI is working on the case."

Two men, Robert Chambliss and Charles Cage, had been arrested earlier and charged with illegal possession of dynamite. They were fined a mere one hundred dollars each and sentenced to 180 days in jail. The irony was that everyone— including the FBI—knew who the bombers were. When the FBI concluded their interviews, they sent a memorandum to FBI director J. Edgar Hoover stating the results of their investigation. They listed four Ku Klux Klansmen as suspects: Robert E. Chambliss, Bobby Frank Cherry, Herman Frank Cash, and Thomas E. Blanton Jr.[4] Most people in the black community thought Hoover tried to block prosecution of the guilty Klansmen, but according to FBI reports, "his concern was to prevent leaks, not to stifle justice. . . . He couldn't have blocked the prosecution and didn't—he simply didn't think the evidence was there to convict."[5]

Sometime in 1968, when I was in college, the FBI officially closed and sealed its investigation, charging no one for the murders. When I learned that the case had been closed and no one had been charged for the deaths of my four friends, I immediately thought about their parents. *What does it feel like to have a daughter violently killed and then, five years later, to have the tragedy practically swept under the rug as if it never happened? How could the white community ignore the cruel injustices and pain suffered by those families?*

That year a reporter with *USA Today* interviewed me about the experience.

"I can describe everything that happened," I told him, "but I cannot tell you the FBI caught the guilty men and brought them to justice. I cannot tell you that officials in Birmingham honored the four girls by naming buildings after them. It seems the girls were just forgotten. Maybe nobody thought my friends' lives were worth bringing the murderers to justice."

⊕

If this tragedy had happened today instead of in 1963, Monday morning would have, no doubt, been set aside as an official day of mourning in Birmingham. City officials would send out teams of crisis counselors to the Birmingham schools to talk with the students and help them cope with their confusion, anger, and grief. Parents would schedule appointments for their children with licensed psychologists and closely monitor them for the days, weeks, and months ahead.

But in 1963, in Birmingham's black community, that didn't happen. On Monday morning, September 16, my brothers and sister and I woke up, dressed in our rooms as always, and then met together in the kitchen to eat. Daddy made a hearty breakfast, like he did every morning. We ate in silence. We left on time for school and work as if nothing had happened the day before. It was as if my four friends were still alive and well and getting ready for school in their own homes.

I felt numb. *What am I supposed to do now? Do churches get bombed and children get killed, and then we all go on living life as usual? Is this just another day in the lives of black people in Birmingham?*

Days passed, and then weeks, and we simply walked through our same routines—predictable schedules disturbed only briefly that Sunday morning.

No one asked me, "Carolyn, are you okay?" "Carolyn, do you miss your friends?" "Carolyn, are you afraid?" "Do you want to talk about what happened at church?"

Nothing was said—not at home and not at school.

⊕

Shortly after the bombing, Reverend C. Herbert Oliver, an African-American pastor in Birmingham, typed out a page-long, single-spaced letter to his fellow members of the Inter-Citizens Committee. The day before, he had telegrammed President Kennedy and listed twenty different, racially motivated, unpunished actions taken by white men against black people in Birmingham. He included the bombings of black homes and businesses, teargassings, shootings, physical violence—all committed against black people between the months of March and September 1963.

Oliver wrote, "The savage, brutal, murderous, and ungodly bombing of Sixteenth Street Baptist Church on Sunday morning, Sept. 14 [sic], has revealed to the whole world the evil of racism. Those few terrifying moments of the blast said what we have been trying to say to the nation for years, that there exists in Alabama the most unconscionable disregard for man and God on the part of some." Oliver continued, "If white supremacy consists in the wanton and brutal destruction of worshippers of God in the very house of worship, then I must confess that the church bombers are the most supreme murderers and cowards the world has ever seen. Only the diseased mind can aspire to reach such depths."

Then the Reverend Oliver described his eyewitness account of the bombing: "On the morning of the bombing I stood across the street from the church behind carbine bearing policemen and watched as the covered bodies were placed into waiting ambulances. Policemen drove a small crowd off the street. I got on a nearby porch. Women seeing the covered bodies being brought from the church cried and screamed without restraint. I could not bring my mind to believe what my eyes saw. It still seems like a tale from some distant land where people know nothing about freedom and democracy."[6]

⊕

I was unusually quiet at school on Monday morning, September 16. When I got there, I laid my head down on my desk. Numb. Confused. Mourning my friends.

Normally I loved school and proved an active, talkative student. But empty desks reminded me again that my friends were dead.

"What's wrong?" a student in the seat in front of me asked.

"I feel bad," I told him. "I don't want to be here."

The student turned around and looked me square in the face.

"I heard about the bombing yesterday, and about the deaths of your friends."

I yearned to hear some words of comfort or consolation from him—from anyone. But that day I received no words of solace, no soothing verbal balm from my schoolmate. He simply said, "Well, frankly, Carolyn, I think you're making more out of this than you should."

I walked through that long school day like a zombie.

CHAPTER 8

THE WORLD WAS SILENT

✦

When you have seen vicious mobs lynch your mothers and fathers at will and drown your sisters and brothers at whim; when you have seen hate-filled policemen curse, kick, and even kill your black brothers and sisters . . . when you suddenly find your tongue twisted and your speech stammering as you seek to explain to your six-year-old daughter why she can't go to the public amusement park that has just been advertised on television, and see tears welling up in her eyes when she is told that Funtown is closed to colored children, and see ominous clouds of inferiority beginning to form in her little mental sky, and see her beginning to distort her personality by developing an unconscious bitterness toward white people . . . when you are forever fighting a degenerating sense of "nobodiness"—then you will understand why we find it difficult to wait.

DR. MARTIN LUTHER KING JR.,
"Letter from Birmingham Jail"[1]

WHEN I WAS SEVEN YEARS OLD, I saw an image on the cover of a magazine that has remained etched in my mind ever since. It was a 1955 edition of *Jet* magazine, a publication primarily designed for black readers, and the photograph on the front showed a dead boy's mutilated head, face, and neck—up close.

I had never seen anything like it before. My heart raced as I thought about each of my four brothers. At fourteen, the boy on the cover wasn't much older than they were, but lying in that coffin, beaten beyond recognition, Emmett Till looked more like a monster than a human being. I stared at the photograph for a long time.

His face was severely swollen. His eyes (what was left of them) looked strange, alien. His misshapen head and discolored skin made him look scary. I found out that Emmett, a youth from Chicago, had traveled to Mississippi to visit relatives in Tallahatchie County. Emmett and some friends had stopped at a market owned by a white man, Roy Bryant, and Emmett had made some boyish and tasteless remarks to Bryant's wife, a clerk at the store. Bryant got angry when he heard about it, and he recruited his half brother, J. W. Milam, to go with him to pay Till a middle-of-the-night visit.

On August 28, 1955, the two men kidnapped Emmett from his bed, drove him to an isolated area, beat and tortured the boy, and shot him in the head. They tied his lifeless body to an old, heavy, factory fan and dumped him in the Tallahatchie River.

Several days later, some boys fishing in the river saw the body and called the police. Officials from the state of Mississippi, where the boy had been murdered, did not even bother to clean up the body of Emmett Till. Debris, dirt, grass, and twigs from the river still stuck to his clothes. They simply stuffed the dead, waterlogged body into a box and nailed it shut. On top of the coffin, they scratched a note: "Do not open." Perhaps they thought the boy's mother would have a quiet funeral and leave the coffin unopened. But she didn't. Outraged over the violent, brutal murder of her son, she ordered the undertakers to leave Emmett's body just as she had received it and to hold an open-casket funeral. She wanted the world to see how her son had suffered and the abuses white murderers had inflicted upon him. Reporters flooded the funeral and made photographs of the dead boy's grotesque face. They published the images in magazines for the whole world to see.

Young Emmett Till might as well have been a dog struck by a car on the highway, its carcass left on the roadside to rot and decay, then picked up and shipped in a box back to its owner. What did this horrifying event say to me, even as a child? That black life is irrelevant, insignificant, worthless. The loss of black life is of no consequence.

Police arrested Bryant and Milam, and the two men faced a trial by jury. It took only sixty-seven minutes for the all-white male jury to find the murderers not guilty. "[We] wouldn't have taken [that] long," one juror admitted, "if [we] hadn't stopped to drink pop."[2] When they heard the verdict, Bryant and Milam smiled, lit up cigars, kissed their wives, and posed for photographers.[3]

Not long after, Bryant and Milam sold their eyewitness confessional story to *Look* magazine for four thousand dollars. They told Alabama journalist William Bradford Huie exactly how they had killed Emmett Till and what they had done with his body.[4] In the article, "The Shocking Story of Approved Killing in Mississippi," Huie quotes Bryant as saying, "That big .45 jumped in Big Milam's hand. The youth [Emmett] turned to catch that big, expanding bullet at his right ear. He dropped."

Bryant and Milam also admitted to pistol-whipping and beating the youth and then rolling him "into 20 feet of water." Huie ended the *Look* article with these haunting words: "The majority—by no means all, but the majority—of the white people in Mississippi 1) either approve of Big Milam's action or else 2) they don't disapprove enough to risk giving their 'enemies' the satisfaction of a conviction."[5]

Such was the plight of black Americans in the United States South at that time. Two white men bragged about killing Emmett Till, a fourteen-year-old boy. Some white men even glorified the killing of black people. And the American people, for the most part, showed no outrage whenever these things happened. They responded with no horror or shock. Just silence. They seemed to accept what had become an everyday occurrence. Usually no one was charged, no one was arrested, no one was punished.

In many ways the article stirred up more emotion across the United States than the murder had. In letters to *Look*'s editors, people wrote,

I want to cancel my subscription to your magazine at once. I will not have my home contaminated with . . . filthy, dishonest articles. (Mrs. W. R. Prevost, Utica, Mississippi)

To publish this story, of which no one is proud, but which was certainly justified, smacks loudly of circulation hunting. Roy Bryant and J. W. Milam did what had to be done, and their courage in taking the course they did is to be commended. To have followed any other course would have been unrealistic, cowardly, and not in the best interest of their family or country. (Richard Lauchli, Collinsville, Illinois)

Some people did respond with outrage at the injustice against Emmett Till. One person wrote,

If this case is not reopened and the guilty punished, I shall laugh at the word "justice." (William T. Bates, Folsom, Pennsylvania)[6]

But other than a few letters to the editor, not much was being done to right this wrong—or prevent it from happening again.

From legal and political standpoints, what happened to Emmett Till was all but swept under the rug for almost fifty years. Finally, on May 10, 2004, the Justice Department reopened the investigation into the murder of Emmett Till, and his body was exhumed, identified, and examined. By then, however, the men who had confessed to his murder had died of cancer—Milam in 1980 and Bryant in 1990.

Incidents like the Emmett Till murder were not limited to Mississippi; acts of racial injustice and violence were happening all over the South. The bombings in Birmingham began the year I was born, 1948. An old steel-producing city—often called the "Pittsburgh of the South"—Birmingham was crisscrossed with made-up racial lines. White families lived on one side of such a line; black families lived on the other side. Until 1948, no one had dared to cross the line. But a few years after World War II, several black families bought houses in a whites-only Birmingham community, and the racial lines became blurred. Some white people—primarily members of the Ku Klux Klan—responded with violence. In an attempt to reestablish the lines that separated black and white communities and to intimidate black residents who crossed over into white neighborhoods, they bombed black homes, businesses, and churches.

Schools weren't immune to the intimidation either. I was nine years old when I sat in front of my family's television set on September 24, 1957, and watched the evening news after President Eisenhower ordered the Arkansas National Guard to escort nine black students into the all-white Little Rock Central High School. I saw crowds of angry, shouting white people—men and women—carrying signs and chanting, "Keep our school white! No n—s in our school!" Their hateful expressions terrified me.

The United States Army's 101st Airborne Division paratroopers accompanied the students while an Army helicopter flew overhead. Then another 350 armed paratroopers circled the school building to protect the black students from violence. The students, dubbed the "Little Rock Nine," made it to class that day—and finished out the entire school year. The following year, Arkansas governor Orval Faubus closed all the high schools. The school board reopened the schools in the fall of 1959.

As I watched the initial forced desegregation, though, several thoughts ran through my mind: *Why are these white people so angry? Why won't they allow black children in their school?* The images on TV frightened me and caused me to ask myself, *Could I do what these black students are doing? Would I have the courage to be one of the first black students in the South to enter an all-white school? Would I be brave enough to stand in the middle of angry white protesters and parents who didn't want me going to their children's school?*

I also wondered why white adults would treat black children so cruelly. It was one thing for black and white *adults* to clash, to fight against each other. But I was surprised to see white adults doing battle against *children*. Even at that age, I knew black children had no power to fight white adults or even to protect themselves from them. I was certain the children would be the ones to suffer in that matchup.

Five years later, on September 30, 1962, I followed another act of school-related terrorism when black student James Meredith enrolled at the University of Mississippi.

Despite the school integration law that had been passed in 1954 as a result of the *Brown v. Board of Education* decision, the university refused Meredith's enrollment, and Governor Ross Barnett tried to block his admission. President John F. Kennedy sent federal marshals to ensure Meredith's right to enroll and to protect him on the campus.

I was fourteen years old when the University of Mississippi confrontation took place. I knew that one day in the near future I, too, would be going to college. My parents and grandparents put a high value on education. Going to college was not an option for me; it was an expectation. Anyway, I was smart, and I looked forward to a college education.

I had seen plenty of discrimination by that point in my life, but I still didn't understand it. *Have people made up their minds that it doesn't matter what the courts decide? Are white people going to maintain the status quo—segregation—regardless of the Supreme Court's ruling? If that is true,* I wondered, *then what do the courts matter—even the United States Supreme Court? What difference does it make what decisions they come to, what laws they pass? Would white people forever be allowed to circumvent the Court's decisions? Would this cycle of segregation repeat itself every time a black person tried to enroll in a white school?* I feared that black children and youth would always be met with the same kind of artillery and white opposition—just for wanting to get a solid education.

I didn't understand it, and I had no answers to my many questions. And in our household, we just didn't talk about what was happening all around us or why it was happening.

⊕

The bombings and terrorism in Birmingham intensified in the early 1960s. *New York Times* columnist and Pulitzer Prize–winner Harrison Salisbury came to my city to investigate the stories of racial violence; he wanted to find out if the rumors were really true. He found his answer.

He wrote that Birmingham was a smoldering volcano of racial tension, "a community of fear."[7] He accused Birmingham of horrible racial cruelties: "Every channel of communication, every medium of mutual interest, every reasoned approach, every inch of middle ground has been fragmented by the emotional dynamite of racism, reinforced by the whip, the razor, the gun, the bomb, the torch, the club, the knife, the mob, the police and many branches of the state's apparatus."[8]

At that time in Alabama, white people lived in their own world, and black people lived in theirs. Black and white did not mix. And neither black nor white understood each other's private worlds.

Birmingham's white society did not like outsiders coming into their city and taking a look around. White Birmingham saw itself as having no problems—in its view, things were moving along just fine. It was true that when the Freedom Riders rode into town, white men beat them up. That was seen as the way of life around here. Most people didn't view it as anything unusual.

But Mr. Salisbury dared to show us the way outsiders saw

FROM MARTIN LUTHER KING JR.'S "LETTER FROM BIRMINGHAM JAIL"

My Dear Fellow Clergymen:

While confined here in the Birmingham City Jail, I came across your recent statement calling my present activities "unwise and untimely." Seldom do I pause to answer criticism of my work and ideas. If I sought to answer all the criticisms that cross my desk, my secretaries would have little time for anything other than such correspondence in the course of the day, and I would have no time for constructive work. But since I feel that you are men of genuine goodwill and that your criticisms are sincerely set forth, I want to try to answer your statements in what I hope will be patient and reasonable terms.

I think I should indicate why I am here in Birmingham, since you have been influenced by the view which argues against "outsiders coming in." I have the honor of serving as president of the Southern Christian Leadership Conference, an organization operating in every Southern state, with headquarters in Atlanta, Georgia. We have some eighty-five affiliated organizations across the South, and one of them is the Alabama Christian Movement for Human Rights. Frequently we share staff, educational and financial resources with our affiliates. Several months ago the affiliate here in Birmingham asked us to be on call to engage in a nonviolent direct-action program if such were deemed necessary. We readily consented, and when the hour came we lived up to our promise. So I, along with several members of my staff, am here because I was invited here. I am here because I have organizational ties here.

But more basically, I am in Birmingham because injustice is here. Just as the prophets of the eighth century B.C. left their villages and carried their "thus saith the Lord" far beyond the boundaries of their home towns: and just as the Apostle Paul left his village of Tarsus and carried the gospel of Jesus Christ to the far corners of the Greco-Roman world, so am I compelled to carry the gospel of freedom far beyond my own hometown. Like Paul, I must constantly respond to the Macedonian call for aid.

Moreover, I am cognizant of the interrelatedness of all communities and states. I cannot sit idly by in Atlanta and not be concerned about what happens in Birmingham. Injustice anywhere is a threat to justice everywhere. We are caught in an inescapable network of mutuality, tied in a single garment of destiny. Whatever affects one directly, affects all indirectly. Never again can we afford to live with the narrow, provincial "outside agitator" idea. Anyone who lives inside the United States can never be considered an outsider anywhere within its bounds.

You deplore the demonstrations taking place in Birmingham. But your statement, I am sorry to say, fails to express a similar concern for the conditions that brought about the demonstrations. I am sure that none of you would want to rest content with the superficial kind of social analysis that deals merely with effects and does not grapple with underlying causes. It is unfortunate that demonstrations are taking place in Birmingham, but it is even more unfortunate that the city's white power structure left the Negro community with no alternative.[9]

our city. He saw the lack of respect white people accorded black people; the exclusiveness of white society; the injustices, mistreatments, and cruelties shown to blacks. What seemed perfectly normal to white Birmingham residents proved a genuine contradiction of our nation's democratic ideals to outsiders such as Salisbury.

Although Salisbury described accurately the terrorism that had become a normal way of life for me, my family, and my community, the article outraged Birmingham's city leaders. It also led to a six-million-dollar libel suit against the *New York Times*—a suit resolved in 1964 in the *Times'* favor.[10]

The belief on the part of white Birmingham residents that life was "perfectly normal" was reflected in the 1961 documentary *Who Speaks for Birmingham?* In it, David Lowe interviewed a leading attorney in Birmingham on the city's race relations. The attorney looked into the television camera and, with serious tone and straight face, said, "Substantially all of the Negroes in Alabama, and perhaps the South, Deep South, have the same background. They were all savages in Africa. Their parents sold them into slavery, or their chieftains sold them into slavery. They were brought into this country in a state of savagery. . . . Their concept, when they were hungry, was to raid the jungles of Africa and to live in the forest."

When David Lowe asked the attorney about court-ordered desegregation of Birmingham's schools and public facilities, the attorney replied, "I don't believe it will ever happen. There would be a measure of violence in Birmingham. . . . There's a lot of white people here that say this: 'Even the dumbest farmer in the world knows that if he has white chickens and black chickens, the black chickens do better if they are kept in one yard to themselves; the white chickens do better if they're kept in a separate yard to themselves.' They each do better under those conditions, and a farmer who would mix white and black chickens would be the dumbest man in the world." During the taped interviews, other leading citizens in Birmingham voiced the same opinions about black people and desegregation.[11]

Whites all over Alabama and the nation seemed to think that the Civil Rights movement was just about sitting next to black people in classrooms or using the same toilets and public facilities. Blacks, however, saw this as a bigger issue. They wanted equal access and opportunities to do whatever their talents and resources would allow them to do. It is one scenario to be unable to attend school for lack of academic standing or financial resources. It is quite another matter to have academic standing and financial resources yet have the door locked and bolted because of one's ethnicity. Blacks wanted life, liberty, and the pursuit of happiness—whatever that meant to each person individually. But in a nutshell, we wanted freedom.

Some blacks were willing to fight for that freedom, and Fred Lee Shuttlesworth was one of them. Sometimes referred to as the "Wild Man from Birmingham," Shuttlesworth has been described as an "unpolished, rabble-rousing Baptist preacher."[12] He and Martin Luther King Jr. had together founded the Southern Christian Leadership Conference, a national Civil Rights group organized after the Montgomery bus boycott. Now, several years later, he felt it was time to contact Dr. King in Atlanta to help him.

Along with most of the black community, I knew who Reverend Shuttlesworth was, and I thought he represented the very height of bravery. To test the 1954 *Brown v. Board of Education* ruling to integrate the public schools, Shuttlesworth had driven to Birmingham's Phillips High School with his two daughters in the car. He planned to enroll them in the all-white school. But white mobs were waiting for him. When he stepped out of his car, white men jumped him. On the evening news, I saw the men hitting and beating and kicking Reverend Shuttlesworth. At the time, I remember thinking, *Surely he knew a white mob was waiting for him at the entrance of Phillips High School that day. But he still drove to the school and got out of his car! Was he afraid of what might happen? Certainly he knew the mob might kill him and his daughters! How in the world did he prepare his mind and heart for that confrontation? What did he tell his daughters might happen? How did he prepare them to possibly meet their deaths?*

I came to see Reverend Shuttlesworth as a minister and a man who was God-sent and who knew what was right. The truth pushed him to fight for the rights of all Birmingham's black people. To me, he was the epitome of courage. Former mayor of Atlanta and U.S. ambassador Andrew Young once described Shuttlesworth as "fearless to the point of insanity."

During those violent years, the Klan bombed Shuttlesworth's home twice and his church once. Very early one Christmas morning as he and his wife lay in bed asleep, an explosion woke him. He opened his eyes, and all he could see was the sky above him. The bomb had blown away the roof of his house and the walls of his bedroom. He figured this close escape from death was God's way of telling him, "Shuttlesworth! I am with you for the duration of this!"

Dr. King accepted Shuttlesworth's invitation to come to Birmingham, a hotbed of racial violence—the city Dr. King called "the most segregated city in America." Together they organized Project C and planned peaceful protests. Dr. King made it clear that any protester confronted with violence by police or the Klan was to respond with nonviolence. Project C officially began on April 3, 1963. I was fifteen years old.

When Bull Connor, Birmingham's commissioner of public safety, heard about the upcoming protests, he obtained a court order forbidding the marches. That meant that if black people marched down the streets of Birmingham, they would be arrested. On Good Friday, April 12, 1963, Dr. King himself was arrested and locked up in a Birmingham jail.

Things in Birmingham certainly heated up when Dr. King arrived. And I was right in the center of it all.

CHAPTER 9

"IT'S TIME!"

⊕

Birmingham is probably the most thoroughly segregated city in the United States. Its ugly record of brutality is widely known. Negroes have experienced grossly unjust treatment in the courts. There have been more unsolved bombings of Negro homes and churches in Birmingham than in any other city in the nation. . . . We have waited for more than 340 years for our constitutional and God-given rights. The nations of Asia and Africa are moving with jetlike speed toward gaining political independence, but we still creep at horse-and-buggy pace toward gaining a cup of coffee at a lunch counter. . . . There comes a time when the cup of endurance runs over, and men are no longer willing to be plunged into the abyss of despair.

DR. MARTIN LUTHER KING JR.,
"Letter from Birmingham Jail"[1]

In January 1963, when newly elected Alabama governor George C. Wallace took the oath of office, he stood proudly before his supporters and, in his inaugural speech, said,

> Today I have stood, where once Jefferson Davis stood, and took an oath to my people. It is very appropriate then that from this Cradle of the Confederacy, this very Heart of the Great Anglo-Saxon Southland, that today we sound the drum for freedom as have our generations of forebears before us done, time and time again through history. Let us rise to the call of freedom-loving blood that is in us and send our answer to the tyranny that clanks its chains upon the South. In the name of the greatest people that have ever trod this earth, I draw the line in the dust and toss the gauntlet before the feet of tyranny . . . and I say . . . segregation today . . . segregation tomorrow . . . segregation forever.[2]

When I heard those painful, frightening words on TV at the age of fourteen, they touched my heart like a hot branding iron. I will never forget them. You see, when white people said things like that, we in the black community knew they would happen. We figured it was settled and that nothing could be done about it. When Wallace announced segregation today, tomorrow, and forever, we just believed that was the way it would always be here in Alabama. I didn't have the maturity or perspective then to know that things can be changed in a society, that segregation wouldn't last forever even though Wallace said it would.

I had never thought much about the "whites only" and "coloreds" signs posted above public facilities. I didn't know why white people drank from one water fountain and black people drank from another fountain or why they used a different toilet. Why did white people sit in the front of city buses and black people sit in the back, behind the signs that said "coloreds"? I didn't know. It was just the way it was. I had grown up with the signs, and I simply obeyed their instructions, as my parents and grandparents had taught me.

It was Dr. Martin Luther King Jr. who first opened my eyes to the injustices that came with segregation and the inhumane treatment of black people in Birmingham. For the first time, I started to think about all those things I had once taken for granted—the way things had always been for black people in Alabama.

Shortly after Dr. King came to Birmingham, I tested the signs for the first and only time in my youth. In the early 1960s, the bus desegregation law had been passed, but the "coloreds" signs still hung prominently in the back of buses. I had seen on television the confrontations between whites and blacks when black people refused to sit in the back of a bus, and I decided I would try it out myself. When I was fifteen years old, I asked my mother, "Mom, do you want me to go downtown to Pizitz department store and pay some money on your bill? It will save you a bus trip." Like many families at that time, we sometimes put clothes on layaway and paid a

FROM GOVERNOR GEORGE WALLACE'S INAUGURAL ADDRESS

The Washington, D.C. school riot report is disgusting and revealing. We will not sacrifice our children to any such type [of] school system—and you can write that down. The federal troops in Mississippi could be better used guarding the safety of the citizens of Washington, D.C., where it is even unsafe to walk or go to a ballgame—and that is the nation's capitol. I was safer in a B-29 bomber over Japan during the war in an air raid, than the people of Washington are walking to the White House neighborhood. A closer example is Atlanta. The city officials fawn for political reasons over school integration and *then* build barricades to stop residential integration—what hypocrisy!

Let us send this message back to Washington by our representatives who are with us today . . . that from this day we are standing up, and the heel of tyranny does not fit the neck of an upright man . . . that we intend to take the offensive and carry our fight for freedom across the nation, wielding the balance of power we know we possess in the Southland . . . that *we*, not the insipid bloc of voters of some sections . . . will determine in the next election who shall sit in the White House of these United States . . . that from this day, from this hour . . . from this minute . . . we give the word of a race of honor that we will tolerate their boot in our face no longer . . . and let those certain judges put *that* in their opium pipes of power and smoke it for what it is worth.

Hear me, Southerners! You sons and daughters who have moved north and west throughout this nation . . . we call on you from your native soil to join with us in national support and vote . . . and we know . . . wherever you are . . . away from the hearths of the Southland . . . that you will respond, for though you may live in the farthest reaches of this vast country . . . your heart has never left Dixieland.

And you native sons and daughters of old New England's rock-ribbed patriotism . . . and you sturdy natives of the great Midwest . . . and you descendants of the far West flaming spirit of pioneer freedom . . . we invite you to come and be with us . . . for you are of the Southern spirit . . . and the Southern philosophy. . . . You are Southerners too and brothers with us in our fight.

What I have said about segregation goes double this day . . . and what I have said to or about some federal judges goes *triple* this day. . . .

And so it was meant in our racial lives . . . each race, within its own framework has the freedom to teach . . . to instruct . . . to develop . . . to ask for and receive deserved help from others of separate racial stations. This is the great freedom of our American founding fathers . . . but if we amalgamate into the one unit as advocated by the communist philosophers . . . then the enrichment of our lives . . . the freedom for our development . . . is gone forever. We become, therefore, a mongrel unit of one under a single all powerful government . . . and we stand for everything . . . and for nothing. . . .

But we warn those, of any group, who would follow the false doctrine of communistic amalgamation that we will not surrender our system of government . . . our freedom of race and religion. . . . That freedom was won at a hard price and if it requires a hard price to retain it . . . we are able . . . and quite willing to pay it.[3]

little money at a time on them. Once the entire bill was paid off, we could take our clothes home.

"Yes, Carolyn," she said. Little did she know I intended to step inside the bus and sit in the front seat!

Quarter in hand, I waited at the stop for the bus to arrive. I was so scared. When the bus came to a halt and the driver swung open the front door, I felt the butterflies in my stomach and dropped my armful of books. Flustered, I jumped up the stairs and tried to get on. I had forgotten to wait and allow the exiting passengers to disembark. The white driver barked at me, "You need to let the people get off the bus before you get on!"

But his reprimand didn't stop me. Instead of backing down the bus stairs, I squeezed inside, pulling close to the rail between the people getting off, and dropped my quarter in the money slot.

My heart beat hard in my chest as I slid into the front seat—the seat where white people always sat. I cut my eyes several times toward the driver as he drove to Pizitz, and I wondered, *Will he say anything to me? Will he make me get up and move to the back of the bus behind the "coloreds" signs?*

Surprisingly, the bus driver said nothing to me as I sat in the white section of his bus. But I was glad when the bus finally arrived at the department store and I could get off.

For the first time in my life, I had deliberately chosen where I wanted to sit, and I hadn't asked anyone for permission. I felt I had won a small battle that day.

✦

I first met Dr. King at my church, Sixteenth Street Baptist, in April of 1963. The church became a central meeting place for Civil Rights leaders to get together and discuss the issues of the day and to plan freedom strategies. As one of the church's hostesses and secretaries, I worked in the office on a regular basis—before and after school, and on weekends—so I had the chance to observe some of these meetings firsthand.

One day, as I was working in the church's back office, I heard singing coming from the sanctuary:

Ain't gonna let nobody turn me around,
Turn me around, turn me around.
Ain't gonna let nobody turn me around,
Keep on a-walking, keep on a-talking.
Gonna build a brand new world.

I had no idea a mass meeting had been scheduled for that day, but a crowd of people had gathered there. As I walked toward the sanctuary, the people continued to sing passionately:

I woke up this morning with my mind (My mind it was)
Stayed on freedom (Oh, well I)
Woke up this morning with my mind
Stayed on freedom (Oh, well I)
Woke up this morning with my mind (My mind it was)
Stayed on freedom.

FROM MARTIN LUTHER KING JR.'S "LETTER FROM BIRMINGHAM JAIL"

In any nonviolent campaign there are four basic steps: collection of the facts to determine whether injustices exist; negotiation; self-purification; and direct action. We have gone through all of these steps in Birmingham. There can be no gainsaying the fact that racial injustice engulfs this community. Birmingham is probably the most thoroughly segregated city in the United States. Its ugly record of brutality is widely known. Negroes have experienced grossly unjust treatment in the courts. There have been more unsolved bombings of Negro homes and churches in Birmingham than in any other city in the nation. These are the hard, brutal facts of the case. On the basis of these conditions, Negro leaders sought to negotiate with the city fathers. But the latter consistently refused to engage in good-faith negotiation.

Then, last September, came the opportunity to talk with leaders of Birmingham's economic community. In the course of the negotiations, certain promises were made by the merchants—for example, to remove the stores' humiliating racial signs. On the basis of these promises, the Reverend Fred Shuttlesworth and the leaders of the Alabama Christian Movement for Human Rights agreed to a moratorium on all demonstrations. As the weeks and months went by, we realized that we were the victims of a broken promise. A few signs, briefly removed, returned; the others remained. . . .

We know through painful experience that freedom is never voluntarily given by the oppressor; it must be demanded by the oppressed. Frankly, I have yet to engage in a direct-action campaign that was "well timed" in the view of those who have not suffered unduly from the disease of segregation. For years now I have heard the word "Wait!" It rings in the ear of every Negro with piercing familiarity. This "Wait" has almost always meant "Never." We must come to see, with one of our distinguished jurists, that "justice too long delayed is justice denied."

We have waited for more than 340 years for our constitutional and God-given rights. The nations of Asia and Africa are moving with jetlike speed toward gaining political independence, but we still creep at horse-and-buggy pace toward gaining a cup of coffee at a lunch counter. Perhaps it is easy for those who have never felt the stinging darts of segregation to say, "Wait." But when you have seen vicious mobs lynch your mothers and fathers at will and drown your sisters and brothers at whim; when you have seen hate-filled policemen curse, kick and even kill your black brothers and sisters; when you see the vast majority of your twenty million Negro brothers smothering in an airtight cage of poverty in the midst of an affluent society . . . when you have to concoct an answer for a five-year-old son who is asking: "Daddy, why do white people treat colored people so mean?"; when you take a cross-country drive and find it necessary to sleep night after night in the uncomfortable corners of your automobile because no motel will accept you; when you are humiliated day in and day out by nagging signs reading "white" and "colored"; when your first name becomes "nigger," your middle name becomes "boy" (however old you are) and your last name becomes "John," and your wife and mother are never given the respected title "Mrs."; when you are harried by day and haunted by night by the fact that you are a Negro, living constantly at tiptoe stance, never quite knowing what to expect next, and are plagued with inner fears and outer resentments; when you go forever fighting a degenerating sense of "nobodiness"– then you will understand why we find it difficult to wait. There comes a time when the cup of endurance runs over, and men are no longer willing to be plunged into the abyss of despair. I hope, sirs, you can understand our legitimate and unavoidable impatience. . . .

I hope the church as a whole will meet the challenge of this decisive hour. But even if the church does not come to the aid of justice, I have no despair about the future. I have no fear about the outcome of our struggle in Birmingham, even if our motives are at present misunderstood. We will reach the goal of freedom in Birmingham and all over the nation, because the goal of America is freedom. Abused and scorned though we may be, our destiny is tied up with America's destiny. Before the pilgrims landed at Plymouth, we were here. Before the pen of Jefferson etched the majestic words of the Declaration of Independence across the pages of history, we were here. For more than two centuries our forebears labored in this country without wages; they made cotton king; they built the homes of their masters while suffering gross injustice and shameful humiliation–and yet out of a bottomless vitality they continued to thrive and develop. If the inexpressible cruelties of slavery could not stop us, the opposition we now face will surely fail. We will win our freedom because the sacred heritage of our nation and the eternal will of God are embodied in our echoing demands.[4]

I stood at the door and looked out over the sanctuary. People packed the main floor and balcony. Most of the people I saw looked like me—about my age, some younger and some older. They were all black. I wasn't surprised, but I didn't quite know what the end would be for this kind of gathering of young people.

Something happened inside me that moment.

I don't know what this is, but I know I want to be part of it. I immediately made up my mind to join them. I went back into the office, put away my work, and walked into the sanctuary. I took a seat on the right side of the church in the middle section. When I looked up, I saw other preachers sitting with Dr. King. I knew all their names, thanks to their media presence: James Bevel, Jesse Jackson, Fred Shuttlesworth, Andrew Young, and Ralph Abernathy.

I had seen Dr. King on television, but I'd never met him. When I saw him in the front of my own church, I thought he looked even more impressive in person. He just had a certain presence. And I was amazed at his gift for oratory. He spoke in a way that made me want to hang onto his every word. I sat spellbound in my pew and soaked it all in. His words seemed to carry me to where he wanted me to be. He spoke on an emotional level—talking about our current living conditions and the things that needed to change. He also spoke on a spiritual level, telling us what freedom could and should look like in our daily lives. He told us that God himself had created the diversity of the universe and that his plan was for unity, not separateness. He said that people had rearranged God's order by segregating the races and that the Civil Rights movement was attempting to restore a rightful order to the universe based on biblical principles.

I never thought about Dr. King's credentials, such as his PhD from Boston University. He was just a good man of God trying to do the right thing. We had been taught to have great respect and reverence for all men of God. I firmly believe that every person of color bearing witness to those events felt that God had called Dr. King and each man at the front of that church to do what they were doing.

Dr. King made me think in ways I had never thought before. He taught that God's plan was for *all* people, not just certain groups of people. God wants us to love our neighbors as he loves us—all our neighbors, whatever their walks in life. Dr. King spoke of the love Paul describes in Romans 13:10—the love that "does no harm to its neighbor." He spoke about the social injustices in our society and the way they mirrored those in the biblical books of Amos, Hosea, Micah, and others.

Even as a teenager, I was convinced that Dr. King was different from other preachers I had heard. Deliberate and purposeful, he addressed us with a calmness, a seriousness, and a serenity I had not heard before from the pulpit. He was grounded, and he knew where he was going. There was no anger or arrogance in his voice, only genuine humility. He was clearly a servant, but he was a leader, too, and something about him touched my heart.

Somehow I knew in my spirit that this was a man called

of God and that God was ordering his steps. I could feel my soul stirring when he spoke. My spirit grew restless, and I knew I had to get involved. Something deep within me wouldn't let me say no.

After Dr. King's speech was over, Reverend Bevel talked about love and nonviolence. He explained that we were fighting for equality, that we should be able to go to state fairs and public libraries and zoos. Something in me resonated with that message. I had always wanted to go to Kiddieland, the city's popular amusement park, but I had never had the opportunity to go.

In the summertime, whenever my parents had driven our car by Kiddieland, I'd look above the tall fence that surrounded the park and see the top of the Ferris wheel going around, with the people—all of them white—strapped in the seats. I'd see the colorful tent top of the merry-go-round, where white children happily sat on horses and traveled in a huge musical circle.

I would lift my ears to the sounds of the festive melodies playing loudly in the background and the noises of crowds of white people having fun and cheering one another in contests. From my backseat car window, I would point my nose toward Kiddieland and breathe in the smells of roasting hot dogs, popcorn, cotton candy, and candied apples cooling on refreshment stand counters. But during my entire childhood, I had seen the amusement park only from the backseat window of our family car as we passed by its beckoning sights, sounds, and smells.

One day I had asked my parents why my brothers and sister and I couldn't go to Kiddieland. They hadn't explained that it allowed only white children and no black kids on its fairgrounds. "You just can't go," my parents had said. When I pressed the issue, my mother had simply told me, "We don't have the money, Carolyn."

I had accepted her answer. *We are poor*, I'd told myself. *That's why we can't go.*

But sitting in the audience as Dr. King spoke that day, I acknowledged a truth that I had known for some time but had carefully avoided: it wasn't about money; it was about skin color.

Some fifteen years later—after I had grown up, gotten married, graduated from Fisk University, and had two daughters of my own—my family and I moved back to Birmingham to live. It was 1978, and that year Birmingham held its annual state fair at Kiddieland. I decided it was high time I made my first visit to the amusement park. My husband, Jerome, and I and our two young daughters drove to the fairgrounds, and I introduced my children to Kiddieland, which like the rest of Birmingham, was technically no longer segregated. I loved the carnival atmosphere that day—and especially eating cotton candy and candied apples. The girls saw cows and horses, and they seemed unusually fascinated by the chickens.

That night, after the girls got settled in their beds, I reflected back on all the times as a child I had yearned to go to Kiddieland but wasn't allowed to because I had black skin. And I felt both sad and happy—sad because I had missed that fun experience as a child but happy because my own daughters could now enjoy it—just as Dr. King had envisioned all those years before.

⊕

At that first meeting at Sixteenth Street Baptist Church, the strategy for the march was clearly laid out. First and foremost, Dr. King insisted that his listeners protest the unfair separateness with love and nonviolence. The agenda for the meeting went something like this:

Welcome/prayer
What we are trying to change
No violent resistance
Rules for marching and participation (no weapons)
Singing/closing

Dr. King spoke as if he were giving a sermon. "If you can't be nonviolent," Dr. King explained, "then you need to find another way to offer your support. The integrity of this movement and march depends on your ability to be non-violent." He gave us these marching instructions: "If someone knocks you down, stay down. Don't resist the dogs. Just stay there. Don't run from them."

At that moment I decided, *If Dr. King is planning a march, I want to march with him!*

Dr. King described in detail what might happen to those of us who joined the march—possible police violence against us, maybe physical injuries, and even the chance of imprisonment. When he had fully explained the risks, he asked the congregation, "Who's willing to stand up for justice, to march for freedom, to take this on?"

The sanctuary grew quiet. Few adults in the church stood up. In those days, an open show of support for Dr. King and the Civil Rights movement could result in the loss of a job—and therefore loss of income for the family's food—or a Klan-planted bomb under a person's home, church, or business. Most of the adults, with good reason, were afraid to risk the little they had worked so hard to gain. They shuddered when they imagined the many ways the white power structure could punish them if they took a visible stand for equal rights. And they remained seated.

But one by one, the young people rose up from their seats and declared their bold commitment in spite of the risks. Schoolchildren, from first graders to high school seniors, stood up straight and tall in the Sixteenth Street Baptist Church sanctuary and offered themselves as "living sacrifices"[5] to the cause of freedom and fairness. And I, at fifteen years old, stood up with them.

That day we were swept up in the spirit of Dr. King's dream—the dream of an undivided Birmingham. If we had to endure pain and imprisonment, we believed it was worth it. In his speech at the Prayer Pilgrimage for Freedom in May 1957, Fred Shuttlesworth had said, "Some of us may have to die to accomplish this [equal rights]." At the time I had thought, *He's not talking about me or about my friends— or other young people. He's talking about the adults who are visibly active in the Civil Rights movement. Only adults die, not kids.* It wasn't until after September 15, 1963, that I finally understood that death could come to any one of us—adults and children alike. Martyrs come in all ages. Some white people in my city were so bent on maintaining segregation that no one was immune from their hate-filled actions.

The leaders gave us no definite date for the march on Birmingham.

"You'll know when it's time," they told us.

From neighborhood to neighborhood and from school to school, black children and youth whispered the plans to one another, made their poster board signs, and waited with excited anticipation.

"Fred Shuttlesworth," one of the ministers said, "you're going to get all of us killed!" But the Fred Shuttlesworth I had come to know and love was fearless. He had been beaten by mobs and thrown in jail, and his house had been bombed. Nothing fazed him.

The youth meetings continued in the church's sanctuary. Sometimes strangers came to the meetings—white infiltrators who wanted to know what we were planning. So we began to speak in a sort of code to keep our plans secret. We listened daily to Shelley Stewart, our favorite radio DJ. He called himself Shelley the Playboy, and speaking in code on the radio, he kept us abreast of the plans to march.

Dr. King warned us again and again of the dangers of marching. "You will encounter the police," he said. "They may hit you or spit on you. They will have dogs and billy clubs." He paused, then continued, "But no matter what the police do to you, the only appropriate response is no response—or a prayerful response."

Dr. King passed around a huge trash can. "When it's time to march, you'll need to get rid of everything that could be perceived as a weapon—nail files, sharp pencils, everything. Get all that stuff off your body."

After we emptied our pockets in preparation for the day of the march, someone a little older than I was came forward and we all sang:

> *Oh freedom!*
> *Oh freedom!*
> *Oh freedom over me.*
> *And before I'll be a slave,*
> *I'll be buried in my grave,*
> *And go home to my Lord and be free.*

Music and singing played a critical role in inspiring, mobilizing, and giving voice to the Civil Rights movement. Dr. King noted that "the freedom songs were playing a strong and vital role in our struggle. They gave the people new courage and a sense of unity." King believed singing kept alive "a faith, a radiant hope, in the future, particularly in our most trying hours."[6] The songs stirred us and got us ready spiritually and emotionally. The lyrics also clearly laid out our strategy: "Ain't Gonna Let Nobody [Bull Connor] Turn Me Around" and "I'm gonna do what the Spirit says do. . . . If the Spirit says march, then march I will." These words settled themselves deep within my spirit, and they live there to this day. When we sang those songs, we believed them, we internalized them, and we were ready to act on them.

We grew excited thinking about the march in downtown Birmingham. "When are we gonna march?" we asked again and again.

"You'll know when it's time," the leaders said.

Many years later, Reverend Shuttlesworth explained to me that the night before the planned march, Dr. King became extremely worried about our safety—most of us were children. He had been criticized with such warnings as, "You're sending children to do the work of adults," and these words haunted him. He decided to call off the march in order to protect us.

"They might get hurt," Dr. King told the other leaders. "Then their parents would be upset and blame us."

The ministers argued among themselves that night—the evening before the march that James Bevel had called D-day. Dr. King was the only one who wanted to cancel; the others wanted to go ahead with it. The young people were eager to finally march. They had been talking excitedly but secretly among themselves for weeks now, and they were ready. They wanted to face the police. They wanted to be arrested. They wanted freedom!

The ministers retired for the night without coming to a consensus. But Bevel had already started the wheels turning. By the time morning broke, there was no turning back.

That morning, May 2, 1963, I woke up and dressed for school as usual. I switched on my radio to WENN and heard DJ Shelley the Playboy announce, "All right, my students! I hope you've got your toothbrushes packed and you're ready!" (Toothbrushes, in code, meant we might spend that night in jail.) We knew what he meant.

Daddy made breakfast that morning as if it were another ordinary day, and after we ate together, the Maull children caught the school bus. But this was no ordinary day. I'd been listening diligently for the DJs code about when the march would take place, and the day had finally arrived. Mama and Daddy and my brothers and sister had no idea that I was going to be part of it. My heart was pounding.

At lunchtime, around eleven o'clock in the morning, students showed up outside the fence at Parker High School carrying big poster boards with large black letters that read, "It's time!"

CHAPTER 10

D-DAY

[We must] use direct action . . . to create a situation so crisis-packed that it will inevitably open the door to negotiation.

DR. MARTIN LUTHER KING JR.,
explaining the purpose of Project C in Birmingham

A handshake is more powerful than a fist.

REVEREND FRED L. SHUTTLESWORTH

It was May 2, 1963. The time to march had come. During morning classes, excited students all over the city began to leave their schools. Some slipped out of windows and jumped to the ground. Many more escaped through front and side doors. I squeezed my skinny body between the school's chain-link fence and padlocked gate. At this point I could feel nothing but adrenaline. It was the first time I had ever left the school grounds without permission. I prayed my father wouldn't find out.

It was finally time to march.

Students from all over Birmingham joined my classmates and me as we walked to Sixteenth Street Baptist Church and Kelly Ingram Park. Some students hiked eighteen miles to join the march. Young people from Miles College arrived in cars and buses. We carried poster board signs, sang "Oh Freedom" at the top of our lungs, and enthusiastically clapped our hands. It seemed like a big pep rally. The police stopped us once and asked us the purpose of the march. Then they told us to disperse. We ran and scattered in different directions, but we all arrived back at the same place: the church corner.

When we reached the church, I stopped and stared. There were white tanks filling Birmingham's bustling streets. Army tanks! No one had said anything about army tanks. They made Birmingham look like a war zone!

Goose bumps of terror rose on my arms. *Are those tanks going to shoot bullets at us, like in a real war?*

But I had no time for fear. Anyway, the friends I had

known all my life—the kids I went to school and church with—stood all around me. They gave me the courage I needed as we continued our march.

I found out later that Bull Connor had ordered the white army tanks onto the streets of downtown Birmingham. If he meant for them to surprise and frighten us, his plan worked.

Then I saw Birmingham firefighters dressed in fire-battling suits and helmets, holding giant hoses. I was confused—there was no fire that I could see, and no one had mentioned anything about water hoses.

Police officers yelled at us through megaphones. "Go home!" they shouted repeatedly. But we didn't listen.

Then they said, "Okay! You have two minutes to disperse!" We continued singing our freedom songs and clapping our hands.

Then came the next shout: "You have one minute!" Again, we ignored them and continued marching.

Finally they started to count: "One! Two! Three! Four! Five! Six! Seven! Eight! Nine! *Ten!*" That didn't stop us either. We were afraid, but we didn't show it.

Bull Connor ran all around us screaming into his megaphone. "Blast them with water!" he shouted to the firefighters.

Upon hearing Connor's order, they turned on the water hoses. It took four strong firefighters to hold one hose. They hit anyone and everyone in their path—most of us were children. This was no longer just a threat; things had escalated to a horrifying new level. I later learned the intense water pressure from one of those hoses could knock the bark off a tree seventy-five feet away. Water shot out at a hundred pounds of pressure per second—hard enough to break bones.

I peeled my eyes away from the firefighters to the police in combat gear. They were struggling to hold back vicious German shepherds on leashes. The dogs snarled and growled, ready to attack upon command. Police paddy wagons lined the streets to haul arrested children to jail.

Hundreds of students were still packed inside the church and thousands more stood outside, waiting to be sent in the next wave of marchers. Each time James Bevel gave the signal, the next group poured out the front door and down the stairs—some fifty children at a time—and continued the peaceful protest march. But despite the intentions of the marchers, I could hardly believe the chaos, confusion, noise, and violence.

Police arrested the first fifty children out of the church for "parading without a permit." These children were stuffed into the paddy wagons and taken to the Birmingham jail. Bevel gave another signal, and fifty more children ran out the church door, down the steps, and into the street. They were laughing, clapping, and singing, "Freedom! Oh freedom!"

Bull Connor shouted more orders. Police arrested students, filled up the paddy wagons, and took them to jail. The children who escaped arrest slipped back into the church. Then they came out the front door again with the next batch of fifty kids.

Moment by moment the waves of marchers continued to pour out onto the street. The children overwhelmed the frustrated Bull Connor. For every child arrested, two more singing and clapping children ran out of the church and started marching. Finally the police had nowhere to put the children they arrested. One of those arrested was my friend and classmate Anita Barnes. There were no more paddy wagons to haul them off to jail. So Bull ordered the city's school buses brought to the church. Police packed bus after yellow school bus with smiling children.

When an embarrassed police department and Bull Connor, Birmingham's commissioner of public safety, saw that they were losing the battle to youngsters, things started getting nasty. "Bring on the dogs!" Connor shouted. The tanks and water hoses frightened me, but the dogs *terrified* me. I was close enough to see that they had teeth like knives. I heard them growl and saw them snap and lunge at fellow marchers—they even tore at the clothes of a couple of people near me. The police, who struggled to maintain their hold on the shepherds' taut leashes, gave attack orders to the animals. The restless dogs charged at anyone close by, grabbed children's arms and legs, bit their stomachs, ripped flesh, and drew significant blood.

As the crowds of children swelled, firefighters continued to aim their thick hoses at the young protestors. I watched in horror while the pressured water sent them flying through the air, knocking them down and pummeling them across the street.

Then, in the heat of the conflict, four firefighters turned their hose on me. Two male students and I were standing in front of a store when suddenly we felt a high-powered blast of water hit us. Our bodies jerked around, and we were pressed tightly against the building. The water struck me like a stinging whip, and I was sure it would knock me down. Many students near me ran away, while others tried desperately to hold on to walls, other people, a ledge—anything. I flattened my body against the brick, steeling myself against the forceful water, and prayed. The pressure of the water blew a hole in my sweater.

Then the firefighters focused the violent stream of water at my face and shoulders. It bruised my face and ripped off a large portion of my hair from the side of my scalp. When we began the march, I was excited—full of hopeful anticipation. I had it in my head that we were going to make a difference. When the fire hoses and dogs came on the scene, I became fearful. By the time I got hit with the water, I was beyond afraid. I was angry. A long time passed, it seemed, before the firefighters turned the hose away from me and directed it onto another child.

I caught my breath and ran through the crowds of children, firefighters, police officers, attack dogs, white tanks, and Bull Connor and found my way into the church basement. I was trembling from head to foot. I had never felt so afraid and angry. Water soaked my clothes. My face and scalp throbbed. I found paper towels and did my best to dry myself off. Then I breathed deeply and struggled to regain some composure.

As I sat in the basement, I listened to the chaos outside. I wanted to go back out there and show my support for Dr. King and the other students. I thought, *But if I do, I'll probably get hurt again—maybe arrested and taken off to jail.*

Actually, I didn't mind getting arrested. But what if I had to telephone my father that night and tell him I was in jail? He had already told me in no uncertain terms, "Don't ever leave the school grounds without permission." At that moment I feared my father's wrath much more than I feared Bull Connor's fire hoses, army tanks, and attack dogs. The risk of arrest and imprisonment seemed trivial compared to facing my father at the end of the day.

I knew Daddy loved me and worried about my safety. I also knew he could lose both his jobs if someone identified his girl-child participating in a public Civil Rights march. So I decided not to return to the streets and to go home instead.

But this led to other problems.

Just how am I going to get home? I decided I had no choice but to walk.

As I headed home, I wondered, *How will I ever explain my appearance—soaked with water, my sweater torn, my hair ruined, and my face bruised—to my dad? There's no way I can explain this to him!*

Maybe, I figured, Daddy would still be at work. I could

slip in, change my clothes, and fix my hair before he got home. Then he'd never know I had marched.

But when I finally got home, I saw Daddy's car parked in front. And someone had locked the screen door, so I couldn't sneak inside. I rang the doorbell and prayed my mother or brothers or sister would answer the door.

That didn't happen. Daddy himself answered the door.

I'm in big trouble now!

Daddy looked at me, wet, bedraggled, and exhausted. His brows drew close together. "Why are you late?" he shouted. "And where have you been?"

I would be grounded forever—I was sure of it. But Daddy had taught me to always tell the truth. So I did.

"I slipped out of school, Daddy. I marched with all the students from the church. We sang 'Freedom! Oh freedom!' and clapped our hands. The police arrested a bunch of my friends. The firemen blasted me with their water hose and tore my sweater. Then I came home."

Daddy said nothing for a long time. My father had seen a lot of pain and injustice in his lifetime. But he never told us children about it. I guess he knew that if a white person hurt me or my brothers or sister, as a black man in Birmingham he couldn't assume the law would do much about it. As expected, Daddy grounded me for good. I was still allowed to go to church events, but he forbade me from doing anything related to the movement.

As I watched the marching scenes on the news that evening, I realized for the first time how serious this was and how badly I could have been hurt. The eyes of the nation were on Birmingham, and I hoped someone would understand what we were trying to do, the message we were trying to send. But it was becoming clear that there could be a high price to pay.

As it turned out, thousands of children had poured from the church that day and marched the streets of Birmingham. Of those children, 959 had been arrested and thrown in jail—one of whom was only four years old! The jails were packed to capacity.[1] Reporters and photographers captured in undeniable images the confrontation between the children and the police. They shot pictures of Bull Connor running around shouting into his megaphone like a well-seasoned war general . . . fighting an army of laughing, dancing children.

It was time to end the silence.

CHAPTER 11

DOUBLE D-DAY

✦

Today was D-day! But tomorrow will be Double D-day!

DJ SHELLEY THE PLAYBOY'S MAY 2 ANNOUNCEMENT
ON BIRMINGHAM'S WENN RADIO

*Bring on your tear gas, bring on your grenades, your new supplies of
Mace, your state troopers and even your national guards. But let the
record show we ain't going to be turned around.*

RALPH ABERNATHY

On the evening of the march, with more than nine hundred arrested children filling Birmingham's jails, Dr. King held a mass church meeting.

"I have been inspired and moved today," he said. "I have never seen anything like it."

The next morning, May 3, hundreds of children skipped school and met again at Sixteenth Street Baptist Church. Bull Connor was waiting for them this time—with squad cars, fire trucks, and water hoses ready. Against threats of violence, the children marched peacefully down the streets of Birmingham.

I was in school this time, per my dad's orders. I didn't want to defy him, and besides, I knew he'd be watching. He was a teacher, and he wouldn't have hesitated to pick up the phone to check on me and make sure I was in school. But I heard later about what happened that day.

Again, Connor ordered the police, "Bring the dogs!" The dogs attacked the protesters—ripping clothes and biting flesh. Connor told the firefighters, "Open up the hoses!" As the water struck the children, they sang one word over and over: "Freedom!" Children knelt on the pavement and prayed while water from fire hoses swept them down the street.

Meanwhile, black and white adults stood along the sidelines and either cheered or booed what they were witnessing. Some onlookers—both black and white—threw bottles and rocks at the police.

As on the day before, hundreds of marching children were arrested on "Double D-day." When the Birmingham jails filled up beyond legal capacity, the school buses delivered the arrested children to the Birmingham fairgrounds—the grounds where Kiddieland was located. It was the first time black children had been allowed inside the fences there. Police locked the children in open hog pens—girls on one side and boys on the other.

For the next two weeks, Connor kept most of the children imprisoned in the jails and in hog pens. Police provided each child with one peanut butter sandwich a day. Horrified parents gathered at the pens and tossed food to their hungry children. In addition to the lack of hot meals, they slept on the filthy ground where state fair animals had been previously housed. The smell was unbearable. They had no private bathrooms, no towels, no change of clothes. When there were thunderstorms, the youngsters got soaked. But their spirits failed to be dampened. Most spent their long hours and days of imprisonment singing and clapping their hands.

"Don't worry about your children," Dr. King told concerned parents. "They're going to be all right. Don't hold them back if they want to go to jail. They are doing a job for all mankind."

Several of my good friends were among those arrested. Thelma Ford, a girl my age who lived five houses down from me, was put in jail on the first day of the march. Her mother had no idea where she was and telephoned my house looking for her. Thelma ended up spending five days in jail.

Two other friends, Sheila Dowdell and James Stewart, were also arrested and put in jail. Sheila's mother had been my fourth grade schoolteacher. James's mother was a teacher, too, and his father was one of the few black doctors in Birmingham. He had a medical office across the street from Parker High School. James's family lived in another part of Birmingham, and James had a swimming pool in his backyard. He often invited us to his house to swim, especially since Birmingham's public pools forbade black youth from using them.

My three friends' parents were able to bail them out, but other children stayed in the hog pens two weeks or more. People around the world heard about the jailed children and sent monetary donations to help pay their bail. And local bondsmen such as Maurice Ryles and Warren King, both of whom lived on my street, assumed responsibility for a number of people who couldn't afford to get out.

Even when it was time for a child to be released, the harassment wasn't over. Connor ordered that each imprisoned child be thoroughly interrogated before he or she could leave. Day after day, officials questioned hundreds of children, one at a time. Officials released the children, even the tiny ones, at random, on their own—and often in the middle of the night. Many parents stayed close to the jail and the fairgrounds so the released youngsters wouldn't have to wander the empty city streets at night trying to find their way home.

By the final tally, after the two days of marching had ended in early May, more than 2,500 people had been arrested. Two thousand of them were children.[1]

After that, the people of Alabama removed Bull Connor

from office. He had served seven terms. It seemed that the children's march was the spark that finally resulted in changed hearts in Birmingham. The shocking images seen all over the world drove people out of their complacency and spurred them to put pressure on leaders in our city. When the news of Bull Connor's removal from office broke, Civil Rights leader Ralph D. Abernathy told those who had marched, "We have already won a victory in Birmingham."

After the children's march, we all gathered in the sanctuary of Sixteenth Street Baptist Church; faced our national flag; put our right hands over our hearts; and as if for the first time, said from the depths of our hearts: "I pledge allegiance to the flag of the United States of America and to the republic for which it stands: one nation under God, indivisible, *with liberty and justice for all.*"

⊕

For the following forty-six years, the state of Alabama refused to erase from its books the names of the two thousand arrested children. The children had official criminal records that followed them throughout adulthood. The state also upheld the fines black people had paid for "parading without a permit."

Then, in August 2009, the city decided to pardon the children who had participated in the 1963 D-day and Double D-day protest.

Most people saw this as progress toward the goal of racial

reconciliation, but I must admit I felt surprised at the city's decision. I've always considered a pardon something one receives after doing wrong. When a person accepts the pardon, it indicates he or she is promising not to repeat the crime. It is like someone saying, "I messed up, and now I want to devote the rest of my life to making it right."

When we marched down the streets of Birmingham in 1963 for our legal rights, we did nothing wrong. We peacefully protested what we believed was right. Years before, the Supreme Court had issued a massive desegregation order for our nation, demanding all public facilities be opened up to everyone, black and white. Governor George Wallace simply said no to the Supreme Court. We were taking a stand against his insistence on a segregated Birmingham—and against the status quo.

In 2009 the city also decided to reimburse all the fines charged to black citizens who had participated in D-day. The fines ranged from one dollar to fifty dollars. The city paid the Reverend Shuttlesworth nine dollars.

⊕

As a teenager, I didn't realize the gravity of what had happened at the children's march in downtown Birmingham. It wasn't until many years later that my eyes were opened to all that had been swirling around me at the time.

First, one of the firefighters who had aimed the water hoses at us on May 2, 1963, came to my church and apologized to the congregation for his part in the violence. He explained that he had been "under orders" and had no choice but to obey Bull Connor. He also told us that the pressure from the hoses had been known to break legs in the past. Thankfully no legs were reported broken throughout the marches. But his talk all those years later was a sobering reminder of how high the stakes had been that day, whether we knew it or not.

Second, I had the privilege of seeing photographs of the event taken by Civil Rights photographer Charles Moore. Several decades after the march, his photographs came out in a book titled *Powerful Days: The Civil Rights Photography of Charles Moore*. In 1996 Mr. Moore came to Birmingham and presented me with a personal copy of his book. Inside, he penned an inscription: "Carolyn, the photograph that I made, on page 99, will always remind me of your courage as a young woman in the front lines of the battle for freedom and justice in 1963 Birmingham. To have met you again in Birmingham in 1968, and in 1996, proved to me that you still have that same spirit and courage. This journalist is proud of all heroes and heroines of Dr. King's Civil Rights movement. With much respect, Charles Moore."

There has been much controversy about who's who in those photos. But to those of us who marched, the pictures are symbolic of all of us and what we endured. The images are reflections of courage—and of our hope for a better Birmingham.

CHAPTER 12

THE MOST DANGEROUS RACIST IN AMERICA

⊕

*[George Wallace is] perhaps the most dangerous racist in America. . . .
I am not sure that he believes all the poison he preaches, but he is artful
enough to convince others that he does.*

DR. MARTIN LUTHER KING JR., INTERVIEW, 1963

*I, George C. Wallace, as Governor of the State of Alabama, have by my
action raised issues between the Central Government and the Sovereign
State of Alabama, which said issues should be adjudicated in the manner
prescribed by the Constitution of the United States; and now being
mindful of my duties and responsibilities under the Constitution of the
United States, the Constitution of the State of Alabama, and seeking
to preserve and maintain the peace and dignity of this State, and the
individual freedoms of the citizens thereof, do hereby denounce and
forbid this illegal and unwarranted action by the Central Government.*

GOVERNOR GEORGE WALLACE[1]

AFTER THE CHILDREN'S MARCH in the streets of downtown Birmingham, Dr. King and the Southern Christian Leadership Conference drew heavy criticism for putting children in harm's way. In the days that followed, however, Dr. King's reputation soared. Shortly after Bull Connor lost his job as commissioner of public safety, the Jim Crow signs came down in my city. Some of Birmingham's public facilities were now open to black people. But desegregation came slowly to Birmingham. George Wallace still fought integration fiercely from the governor's office, claiming each state should have the right to decide what was best for its citizens.

"Segregation today! Segregation tomorrow! Segregation forever!" he had promised the white people of Alabama earlier that January. And he meant it.

Wallace told his supporters that he'd physically block schoolhouse doors rather than allow black children and youth to enroll into Alabama's all-white public schools and state colleges.

What makes him hate black people so much? I wondered at the time. It didn't really occur to me that he would carry out his commitment so literally.

But one month after the children's march, that's exactly what George Wallace did. When a federal judge ordered the University of Alabama in Tuscaloosa to register and enroll two Alabama-born black students, Vivian Malone and James Hood, Wallace placed his body in front of the Foster Auditorium door and physically kept them from entering.

June 11, 1963, three months before the church bombing,

proved a typical sweltering summer day in Alabama. Crowds of cheering and sweating white supporters and national news reporters filled the campus. Television cameras rolled. Alabama state troopers surrounded Wallace as he made his defiant stand against desegregation in Alabama's all-white public schools. Wallace claimed it was his state's constitutional right, not the federal government's right, to operate Alabama's public schools, colleges, and universities. The *Tuscaloosa News* reported later that the governor "squeezed every suspenseful moment of drama from the occasion."[2]

President Kennedy had anticipated Wallace's stand and in response sent Deputy Attorney General Nicholas Katzenbach and a swarm of federal marshals to Tuscaloosa. Katzenbach told Wallace, loud enough for all to hear, to abide by the federal court order. "From the outset, Governor," Katzenbach said, "all of us have known that the final chapter of this history will be the admission of these students."[3]

When ordered to "step aside and let the black students enter the university," Wallace refused to move. Katzenbach telephoned President Kennedy, who immediately federalized the Alabama National Guard. Wallace then had no choice. He reluctantly stepped aside.

That evening on national television, my family and I watched a distressed United States president address the nation:

"I hope that every American, regardless of where he lives, will stop and examine his conscience about this and other related incidents," John F. Kennedy said. "This Nation was founded by men of many nations and backgrounds. It was founded on the principle that all men are created equal, and that the rights of every man are diminished when the rights of one man are threatened."

Here is a powerful white man, I thought as I listened, *the leader of our nation, standing up for the rights of my people!*

"It ought to be possible," Kennedy continued, "for American students of any color to attend any public institution they select without having to be backed up by troops."

Does this mean I'll actually have the choice to go to a white college—anywhere I choose? I wondered.

"It ought to be possible for American consumers of any color to receive equal service in places of public accommodation, such as hotels and restaurants and theaters and retail stores, without being forced to resort to demonstrations in the street," the president stated, "and it ought to be possible for American citizens of any color to register to vote in a free election without interference or fear of reprisal."

You mean I could walk up the grand stairway at Pizitz department store and order a hot dog, French fries, and a Coke in the mezzanine café? I marveled to myself. *And the waitress will, by law, have to serve me?*

"It ought to be possible, in short, for every American to enjoy the privileges of being American without regard to his race or his color. In short, every American ought to have the right to be treated as he would wish to be treated, as one would wish his children to be treated," Kennedy said. "But this is not the case."

At that moment, I loved and admired the president even more than before.

He and his brother Bobby Kennedy seemed to genuinely care about people of color. As I listened to my president talk to the nation about segregation and its unfairness to black people, I thought, *Here is a president who understands. Maybe he'll do something about all this mess! Maybe I could even go to the University of Alabama or Howard College or even an Ivy League School!*

That evening President Kennedy told the nation that one hundred years of delay had passed since President Lincoln freed the slaves and that their heirs weren't yet fully free from injustice, social discrimination, and economic oppression.

Then he added, "And this Nation, for all its hopes and all its boasts, will not be fully free until all its citizens are free."

As I listened to the president's powerful speech on Civil Rights, I felt a sense of great relief and sudden hope. My people had been wronged, and now somebody in an important position was finally coming alongside to offer us some support.

The president can make people change, I figured. *Black people can't tell white people what to do. But if Kennedy, a white man—the president of the United States—says that things need to change, surely white people will listen to him.*

My family and I stayed glued to the television that night. Excitement and hope swelled in our hearts. Kennedy told the nation that segregation was a moral issue—"as old as the Scriptures and . . . as clear as the American Constitution."

FROM JOHN F. KENNEDY'S CIVIL RIGHTS ADDRESS

This afternoon, following a series of threats and defiant statements, the presence of Alabama National Guard was required
on the University of Alabama to carry out the final and unequivo-
cal order of the United States District Court of the Northern
District of Alabama. That order called for the admission of two
clearly qualified young Alabama residents who happened to have
been born Negro. That they were admitted peacefully on the
campus is due in good measure to the conduct of the students
of the University of Alabama, who met their responsibilities in a
constructive way.

I hope that every American, regardless of where he lives, will
stop and examine his conscience about this and other related
incidents. This Nation was founded by men of many nations and
backgrounds. It was founded on the principle that all men are
created equal, and that the rights of every man are diminished
when the rights of one man are threatened. . . .

This is not a sectional issue. Difficulties over segregation and
discrimination exist in every city, in every State of the Union,
producing in many cities a rising tide of discontent that threatens
the public safety. Nor is this a partisan issue. In a time of domestic crisis men of good will and generosity should be able to unite
regardless of party or politics. This is not even a legal or legisla-
tive issue alone. It is better to settle these matters in the courts
than on the streets, and new laws are needed at every level,
but law alone cannot make men see right. We are confronted
primarily with a moral issue. It is as old as the Scriptures and is
as clear as the American Constitution.

The heart of the question is whether all Americans are to be afforded equal rights and equal opportunities, whether we are going to treat our fellow Americans as we want to be treated. If an American, because his skin is dark, cannot eat lunch in a restaurant open to the public, if he cannot send his children to the best public school available, if he cannot vote for the public officials who will represent him, if, in short, he cannot enjoy the full and free life which all of us want, then who among us would be content to have the color of his skin changed and stand in his place? Who among us would then be content with the counsels of patience and delay?

One hundred years of delay have passed since President Lincoln freed the slaves, yet their heirs, their grandsons, are not fully free. They are not yet freed from the bonds of injustice. They are not yet freed from social and economic oppression. And this Nation, for all its hopes and all its boasts, will not be fully free until all its citizens are free.[4]

Then he asked a question I will never forget: "Who among us would be content to have the color of his skin changed and stand in his place? Who among us would then be content with the counsels of patience and delay?"[5]

Maybe things will change here in Alabama!

Some things did change in my city. At the end of July I dressed up in my freshly starched white Sunday dress and slipped on my shiny black patent-leather church shoes. With my head held high, I walked to the Pizitz department store in downtown Birmingham. I saw the white people eating in the mezzanine's café at the top of the grand spiral staircase. I smelled the food. I slowly and gracefully climbed the stairs, entered the café, and sat down at a table. Then I ordered a hot dog, French fries with ketchup, and a Coke.

This might seem like a small thing to some people, I thought as I sipped my Coke and paid the bill. *But it's a big deal to me!*

That day I also thought about my grandmother and her final days in the Princeton Hospital. *Maybe now, Mama Lessie, no other black child's beloved grandmother will have to die beneath the dripping water pipes in a cold, dingy hospital basement.*

Students James Hood and Vivian Malone eventually were admitted into the University of Alabama,* but George Wallace refused to accept defeat. Nothing and no one—not even the president of the United States—would thwart

---

* James Hood left the university after only two months, wanting to avoid a breakdown. He did return in 1995, however, to earn his doctorate degree. On May 30, 1965, Vivian Malone became the first black student to graduate from the University of Alabama in its 134 years of existence. But her path there was not easy. One night someone knocked on her dormitory door and warned her of a bomb threat. No bomb materialized, but that November, three bombs exploded at the university, one of them just blocks from her dormitory.

Wallace's plan for continued segregation in Alabama's public schools and universities.

Less than three months later, on September 9, 1963, Governor Wallace signed Executive Order Number Ten of the Governor of Alabama. "Whereas," Wallace began, "the threat of forced and unwarranted integration of the public schools of this State is detrimental to the public interest; and, whereas, integration . . . will totally disrupt and effectively destroy the educational process and constitutes an abridgment of the Civil Rights of other children attending the schools, and deprives them of the equal protection of the laws and constitutes the deprivation of their rights, liberty and property without due process of law . . ." Wallace closed the executive order with a final paragraph: "Now, therefore, I, George C. Wallace, as Governor of the State of Alabama, and in conformity with the Constitutional and statutory power vested in me as Governor of said State, do hereby order and direct that no student shall be permitted to integrate the public schools of the City of Birmingham, Alabama."[6]

In response, on that same day, President Kennedy issued a report on desegregation in the schools of Alabama. "It should be clear," Kennedy wrote, "that United States Government action regarding the Alabama schools will come only if Governor Wallace compels it."

In 144 school districts in eleven Southern and border states, desegregation happened in a peaceful manner, with no need for the federal government to intervene. But in

FROM PRESIDENT JOHN F. KENNEDY'S REPORT ON DESEGREGATION IN THE SCHOOLS OF ALABAMA

In 144 school districts in 11 Southern and border States, desegregation was carried out for the first time this month in an orderly and peaceful manner. Parents, students, citizens, school officials, and public officials of these areas met their responsibilities in a dignified, law-abiding way. It wasn't necessary for the Federal Government to become involved in any of those States.

In the State of Alabama, however, where local authorities repeatedly stated they were prepared to carry out court directives and maintain public peace, Governor Wallace has refused to respect either the law or the authority of local officials. . . .

This Government will do whatever must be done to see that the orders of the court are implemented—but I am hopeful that Governor Wallace will enable the local officials and communities to meet their responsibilities in this regard, as they are willing to do.[7]

Alabama, Kennedy noted, "Governor Wallace has refused to respect either the law or the authority of local officials."

Kennedy ended his report with the hope that Governor Wallace would comply with the desegregation order, but also the promise that the U.S. government would take whatever steps necessary to intervene should he decide not to.[8]

George Wallace responded to the president's report. He told the *New York Times* that, in order to stop school integration, Alabama needed "a few first-class funerals."[9] Wallace got his "first-class funerals" less than three months later—Cynthia, Denise, and Addie's and Carole's.*

But the battle for desegregation in Alabama schools was only heating up. The school desegregation laws established in 1954 were little more than a piece of paper in Alabama because, thus far, nothing had changed. Some people would end up paying a dear price for their courageous stands against Governor Wallace and the Ku Klux Klan before the dust finally settled.

---

* In October 1996 former governor Wallace, in poor health, met with Vivian Malone and James Hood and apologized for his actions at the University of Alabama. Wallace admitted that his actions were wrong and that the state of Alabama was better as a result of the integration of the schools. When Wallace presented Vivian with the Lurleen B. Wallace Award for Courage (named for Wallace's wife), the two of them reconciled and spoke of forgiveness.

CHAPTER 13

THE BATTLE CONTINUES

I have a dream that one day the state of Alabama, whose governor's lips are presently dripping with the words of interposition and nullification, will be transformed into a situation where little black boys and black girls will be able to join hands with little white boys and white girls and walk together as sisters and brothers.

DR. MARTIN LUTHER KING JR.,
"I Have a Dream"

All this will not be finished in the first 100 days. Nor will it be finished in the first 1,000 days, nor in the life of this administration, nor even perhaps in our lifetimes on this planet. But let us begin.

JOHN F. KENNEDY

ON THE DAY AFTER GEORGE WALLACE made his public stand in the University of Alabama's doorway and President Kennedy spoke on television to the nation about Civil Rights, a member of the Klan shot and killed black Civil Rights leader Medgar Evers, the field secretary for the National Association for the Advancement of Colored People (NAACP).

Evers had attracted national attention back in the early 1960s when he led a store boycott in Jackson, Mississippi, and when he helped black student James Meredith enter the all-white University of Mississippi in 1962. As Evers pulled into the driveway of his home in Jackson, Mississippi, white supremacist and Klan member Byron De La Beckwith was hiding, waiting for Evers to step out of his car. Then, with Evers's wife and young children watching, De La Beckwith shot him in the back. Evers died that night in his driveway.

When I heard about the assassination that evening on the television news, I worried about my own dad driving home from work. *Will someone shoot Daddy in the back and leave him to die in our driveway?* I wondered. But I didn't talk to anyone about my fears. I kept them bottled inside, hidden away from my parents and my friends.

Even at that young age, I knew I couldn't trust the legal system to bring about justice. Byron De La Beckwith was arrested, tried, and acquitted by an all-white jury. It was the verdict we'd expected. He went free for the next thirty-one years.[*]

---

[*] In 1994 assistant district attorney Bobby DeLaughter reopened the Evers case. In the retrial, the jury convicted and imprisoned De La Beckwith for the murder of Medgar Evers.

→ Me at age two with my aunt Maxine in front of our house in Birmingham.

Me at age nine in my third-grade school photo. ←

Me at age two (on the right, with one shoe), playing with friends in our front yard. ↓

Standing in front of my granddaddy's house at age thirteen with my cousin Deloris (on the left) and my granddad, Rev. E. W. Burt.

Taken on my graduation day from A. H. Parker High School, May 1965.

Me during my freshman year at Fisk University.

→ With my husband, Jerome, on Christmas Day 2002.

With Condoleezza Rice at an event in Duluth,
Georgia, in April 2008. →

With Jimmy Carter at the Birmingham Civil Rights
Institute in January 2009. ↑

🌿 I lost my friends (from left) Denise McNair, 11; Carole Robertson, 14; Addie Mae Collins, 14; and Cynthia Wesley, 14, at 10:22 a.m., September 15, 1963.

🌿 A civil defense worker and firefighters walk through the debris following the explosion at the Sixteenth Street Baptist Church.

➤ Police officers stand guard outside the Sixteenth Street Baptist Church after the bombing. The explosion did extensive damage to the church and shattered the face of Jesus in the stained-glass window seen in the background.

✤ Flowers cover the caskets of Denise McNair, Addie Mae Collins, and Cynthia Wesley as funeral services are held at the Sixth Avenue Baptist Church on September 18, 1963.

Mourners who overflowed the church stand across the street during funeral services for 14-year-old Carole Robertson, September 17, 1963. ✤

→ A friend wipes tears from the face of Mrs. Lorene Ware during funeral services for her son Virgil Lamar Ware, September 22, 1963, in Birmingham. Virgil was killed during one of several racially motivated incidents that occurred immediately following the Sixteenth Street Baptist Church bombing.

A seventeen-year-old ← demonstrator is attacked by a police dog during a Civil Rights march in Birmingham, May 1963.

→ The Birmingham Fire Department aims high-pressure water hoses at several student marchers during Dr. Martin Luther King's children's march in May 1963.

Dr. Martin Luther ←← King Jr. addresses marchers during his famous "I Have a Dream" speech at the Lincoln Memorial in Washington, D.C., August 28, 1963.

←← Robert F. Kennedy uses a bullhorn to address black demonstrators speaking out for equal rights on June 14, 1963.

Dr. Martin Luther ←← King Jr. (left), Rev. Fred Shuttlesworth, and Rev. Ralph Abernathy hold a news conference in Birmingham on May 8, 1963.

⚜ This stained-glass window was given to the Sixteenth Street Baptist Church in 1965 by the people of Wales following the bombing.

That incident set something off inside me—it seemed even more horrific than the other racially motivated murders that had happened recently throughout the South. I was starting to grasp how little value black people had in my country, and I knew it wasn't right. *We aren't considered "real people" who have feelings and dreams and ambitions—people who want the best for their children*, I railed to myself. *Is anybody going to stand up and say, "This is wrong! We're going to bring justice to this situation!"*

I started to worry even more about my own family after Evers's death—especially my father and four brothers. It seemed so scary to me—a man shot in the back at night, unable to defend himself, with his family watching him die in his own driveway. *Surely*, I thought, *this is the epitome of evil: Byron De La Beckwith.*

⊕

In the midst of all the hype surrounding school desegregation, I was beginning to think seriously about where I wanted to go to college myself within the next few years.

I had always been an A student, and I loved reading and learning. The expectation from my parents and my teachers alike was that college would be a given for me. From the time I was in elementary school, my teachers saw my spelling potential—already at a twelfth grade level, according to the California Achievement Tests—and they asked my parents if they could help me develop it. For two years, from the sixth grade to the eighth grade, from two o'clock to three o'clock each school day, my teachers took me to the teachers' lounge and individually worked with me on my spelling skills.

I felt privileged to be allowed in an area that was typically off-limits to other students. Sometimes, however, I got so sick of spelling and spelling books that I cried. When that happened, one of my teachers would tell Miss Pullum—the lady who supervised our school cafeteria—to give me some ice cream. The choices were chocolate, vanilla, or strawberry. I always chose my favorite—chocolate. The ice cream came with a small wooden spoon wrapped in thin white paper. Other times one of the teachers would give me a quarter to buy a Coca-Cola. In those days, buying a Coke was a big treat—we seldom had Coke at home.

When I was a seventh grade student at Finley Avenue Elementary School, Mr. A. G. Gaston held a spelling bee for Birmingham's black students. I entered the contest, and with more than four hundred other students participating, I won first place—out of my city, county, and state. While I was there, I met a fellow contestant, Mary Kate Bush, who later became a great source of strength to me, as well as a lifelong friend. In fact, Mary Kate became my roommate at Fisk University.

I was given a trophy with my name and my school's name on it, and my photo appeared in the *Birmingham News* on May 7, 1961, with the caption "Birmingham Girl Winner of Gaston Spelling Bee." Somewhere in a Birmingham school, a Gaston Spelling Bee trophy with the words *Carolyn Jean*

Maull engraved on the front sits entombed in a glass cabinet. I still wonder if I could have won the National Spelling Bee competition if black students had been allowed to compete.

My parents were proud of me. But one omission in the local newspaper article upset my father. The reporter had listed me as the daughter of Mrs. Ernestine Maull and made no mention of my dad. It upset him because so many black children at that time had no fathers in their homes, and he wanted everyone to know I had a father.

⊕

I have often wondered what I might have become in life had society's doors been more open to me—a child and youth of color—in the 1950s and 1960s. What path might I have walked if more opportunities had been available to me in Birmingham? What exciting turns would my life have taken if I had been as unhindered in my decision making as Alabama's white children and youth?

"Carolyn," Mama and Daddy suggested when I started thinking about my options for college, "please consider Fisk University in Nashville. Fisk is an all-black school. That'll be easier. You certainly don't want to go through what Vivian Malone or James Hood endured to go to college! You will face enough challenges at Fisk University, but the color of your skin won't be one of them."

Fisk University had been founded barely six months after the end of the Civil War and just two years after the

FROM MARTIN LUTHER KING JR.'S "WHERE DO WE GO FROM HERE?" SPEECH

In assault after assault, we caused the sagging walls of segregation to come tumbling down. During this era the entire edifice of segregation was profoundly shaken. This is an accomplishment whose consequences are deeply felt by every southern Negro in his daily life. It is no longer possible to count the number of public establishments that are open to Negroes. Ten years ago, Negroes seemed almost invisible to the larger society, and the facts of their harsh lives were unknown to the majority of the nation. But today, civil rights is a dominating issue in every state, crowding the pages of the press and the daily conversation of white Americans. In this decade of change, the Negro stood up and confronted his oppressor. He faced the bullies and the guns, and the dogs and the tear gas. He put himself squarely before the vicious mobs and moved with strength and dignity toward them and decisively defeated them. And the courage with which he confronted enraged mobs dissolved the stereotype of the grinning, submissive Uncle Tom. He came out of his struggle integrated only slightly in the external society, but powerfully integrated within. This was a victory that had to precede all other gains.

In short, over the last ten years the Negro decided to straighten his back up, realizing that a man cannot ride your back unless it is bent. We made our government write new laws to alter some of the cruelest injustices that affected us. We made an indifferent and unconcerned nation rise from lethargy and subpoenaed its conscience to appear before the judgment seat of morality on the whole question of civil rights. We gained manhood in the nation that had always called us "boy." . . . But in spite of a decade of significant progress, the problem is far from solved. The deep rumbling of discontent in our cities is indicative of the fact that the plant of freedom has grown only a bud and not yet a flower. . . .

With all the struggle and all the achievements, we must face the fact, however, that the Negro still lives in the basement of the Great Society. He is still at the bottom, despite the few who have penetrated to slightly higher levels. Even where the door has been forced partially open, mobility for the Negro is still sharply restricted. There is often no bottom at which to start, and when there is there's almost no room at the top. In consequence, Negroes are still impoverished aliens in an affluent society. They are too poor even to rise with the society, too impoverished by the ages to be able to ascend by using their own resources. And the Negro did not do this himself; it was done to him. For more than half of his American history, he was enslaved. Yet, he built the spanning bridges and the grand mansions, the sturdy docks and stout factories of the South. His unpaid labor made cotton "King" and established America as a significant nation in international commerce. Even after his release from chattel slavery, the nation grew over him, submerging him. It became the richest, most powerful society in the history of man, but it left the Negro far behind.

And so we still have a long, long way to go before we reach the promised land of freedom. Yes, we have left the dusty soils of Egypt, and we have crossed a Red Sea that had for years been hardened by a long and piercing winter of massive resistance, but before we reach the majestic shores of the promised land, there will still be gigantic mountains of opposition ahead and prodigious hilltops of injustice. We still need some Paul Revere of conscience to alert every hamlet and every village of America that revolution is still at hand. Yes, we need a chart; we need a compass; indeed, we need some North Star to guide us into a future shrouded with impenetrable uncertainties.

Now, in order to answer the question, "Where do we go from here?" which is our theme, we must first honestly recognize where we are now. When the Constitution was written, a strange formula to determine taxes and representation declared that the Negro was sixty percent of a person. Today another curious formula seems to declare he is fifty percent of a person. Of the good things in life, the Negro has approximately one half those of whites. Of the bad things of life, he has twice those of whites. Thus, half of all Negroes live in substandard housing. And Negroes have half the income of whites. When we turn to the negative experiences of life, the Negro has a double share: There are twice as many unemployed; the rate of infant mortality among Negroes is double that of whites; and there are twice as many Negroes dying in Vietnam as whites in proportion to their size in the population.

In other spheres, the figures are equally alarming. In elementary schools, Negroes lag one to three years behind whites, and their segregated schools receive substantially less money per student than the white schools. One-twentieth as many Negroes as whites attend college. Of employed Negroes, seventy-five percent hold menial jobs. This is where we are.

Where do we go from here? First, we must massively assert our dignity and worth. We must stand up amid a system that still oppresses us and develop an unassailable and majestic sense of values. We must no longer be ashamed of being black. The job of arousing manhood within a people that have been taught for so many centuries that they are nobody is not easy.[1]

Emancipation Proclamation, primarily to educate freedmen and the biracial, light-skinned children born to white slave owners who had impregnated their female slaves. These children, half-white and half-black, fit into neither white nor black society in the South.

Our society still had a long way to go, of course, but in the early days of September 1963, I felt a genuine hope about the future—about things improving between the races in Alabama. I was smart, talented, and I loved my school and church. I had my family and lots of good friends. I missed Mama Lessie, but I still had my wonderful granddaddy. I had matured listening to the words of my pastor, of Dr. Martin Luther King Jr., and of others that year. I was proud that I had participated in the Civil Rights movement, singing freedom songs and marching peacefully with my friends. Life was good. And I felt certain that things in Birmingham were finally changing for the better.

❖

That sense of well-being was shattered the instant the bomb went off that Sunday morning in September 1963—the day I grew up. I've learned in the years since that some moments in history and in our lives go away. The issues we understand easily and the fears we resolve quickly fade into the past. They get filed away into a memory cabinet marked "closed."

Other events, however, refuse to go away. They become a part of our "forever" thoughts, and they surface unexpectedly at the most unpredictable times. These memories can be painful, but perhaps some things should never go away— they should be kept in the forefront of our minds to provide continuing lessons for daily life.

Whatever excitement and girlish joy I felt before the bombing simply died for a long period after the bombing. My heart built a barrier that sealed off my hope, my happiness, and my very soul, just like the wall the church had built to seal off the restroom where the four girls perished. A dark cloud formed above my head and became my constant, unwanted companion. It followed me everywhere I went. It was like my life-changing baptism two years before—only a different kind of baptism. "Dead and buried," but seemingly with no hope for a future "resurrection." I had lost hope in my white fellow human beings.

CHAPTER 14

SERVANT, HEAL THYSELF

⊕

I have seen us come so far, but we have so much farther to go.

REVEREND FRED L. SHUTTLESWORTH,
at his eightieth birthday celebration with Civil Rights leaders, 2002[1]

Life is hard, at times as hard as crucible steel. It has its bleak and difficult moments. Like the ever-flowing waters of the river, life has its moments of drought and its moments of flood. Like the ever-changing cycle of the seasons, life has the soothing warmth of its summers and the piercing chill of its winters. And if one will hold on, he will discover that God walks with him, and that God is able to lift you from the fatigue of despair to the buoyancy of hope, and transform dark and desolate valleys into sunlit paths of inner peace.

MARTIN LUTHER KING JR.,
funeral service for Addie Mae Collins, Denise McNair, and Cynthia Diane Wesley[2]

IN THE DAYS THAT FOLLOWED SEPTEMBER 15, 1963, sadness consumed me. The smile left my face. Joy faded from my heart. I felt depressed all the time, plagued by a general hopelessness. Even though it seemed a logical conclusion, I never connected my newfound sadness and depression with my friends' violent deaths. At the time, I had no knowledge of the grief process, clinical depression, or survivor's guilt syndrome. Those were not the days of trauma teams and school grief counseling—especially not for black people.

The dark cloud tormented me day and night. I had trouble sleeping, yet that is all I wanted to do. When I did fall asleep at night, it hurt to wake up in the mornings. The excitement I had once felt about school and learning simply went away. Deep down I was afraid for my safety—terrified of getting my head blown off, like Cynthia had, in a Klan explosion.

With the passage of time, as well as a somewhat closed-off memory, I managed to live a perfunctory life. I have little recollection of the days that followed September 15, 1963. I guess everyone settled into the regular tasks of autumn. Children went to their schools. Adults went to their jobs. Sixteenth Street Baptist Church underwent renovations, and most of our members met weekly for worship at the nearby L. R. Hall Auditorium. Some people felt too afraid to come back and left our congregation for good. Either they stopped going to church altogether or they joined other churches in the city. Church records placed membership numbers over eight hundred before the bombing; after the bombing, that number shrank by 50 percent.

Tension and fear continued to stalk our city. We knew the rules had changed. Our neighborhoods had been bombed before, but no one had ever been killed. Until now. The message gnawed away at the corners of our hearts: "You can kill black people. It's okay, because even if someone is arrested, no one goes to jail for it." Black life was cheap.

Ten days after the church bombing, on September 25 at 2:31 a.m., another bomb exploded in a nearby black neighborhood. The blast brought a number of police officers to the area to search for the bomb site. Fortunately, they failed to find it. Thirteen minutes after the first bomb exploded, another bomb went off at the same spot. A shrapnel bomb, they called it—several sticks of dynamite in a rusty five-gallon paint can crammed full of nails, bolts, and sharp pieces of metal.

Birmingham residents had once believed Klan bombs were meant only to intimidate people, not kill people. The shrapnel bomb changed all that.[3]

I noticed with fresh awareness the real powerlessness of the black community. Some people became unusually quiet and accommodating, not daring to rock the boat. Others became the opposite—outspoken and militant against the inhumane treatment of the city's (and nation's) black citizens.

That autumn and winter, I just wanted to be alone. I often found a lonely corner in my house, sat down, and wrapped my arms tightly around my body. Then, in an effort to bring myself some comfort, I rocked back and forth, hugging myself, trying to make the deep pain go away.

I don't remember having a preoccupation with death

and dying before the bombing. I'd always been a carefree kid—I loved to skate and play marbles. Very few girls I knew played marbles, let alone had a special marble collection like I did. But after the church bombing, nothing seemed the same anymore, including the way I viewed myself, others, and the world.

But hope wasn't completely lost. The black people in Birmingham still had two "saviors" who continued to share our dreams for a more promising future: President John F. Kennedy and Dr. Martin Luther King Jr. Our hope was kept alive through their championing efforts. As a community, we placed our trust in their ability to somehow keep Klan bombs from killing our loved ones and destroying our homes and churches.

Back in 1960, I had felt a surge of hope when John F. Kennedy became president of the United States. I watched him on TV as he addressed the nation and Jackie Kennedy as she gave a White House tour. I laughed when I saw little Caroline run on the beach in a tiny swimsuit and when John John paraded around his father's Oval Office in his sailor suit. I just wished Mama Lessie had lived to see these things.

I was filled with eager anticipation when a pregnant Jackie left for the hospital to deliver her third child. And I remember crying when, on August 10, 1963, three-day-old Patrick Bouvier Kennedy died. I watched the Kennedys grieve over their dead child just as anybody else would.

Even though the Kennedys reigned like a king and queen

in our country, I saw something in them that appeared normal and everyday. They seemed like a down-to-earth family who, in spite of wealth and fame, really cared about people. They weren't preoccupied, as part of our nation seemed to be, with race and skin color.

John F. Kennedy gave me tremendous hope for a different future for black people in Alabama. I remember something my father said after hearing Kennedy's speech on TV following the children's march: "I think he [Kennedy] is a good man." We saw that our president wanted to do the right thing for black people, and it gave us faith. Sometimes people don't know what justice and freedom look like. It took the president's going on national television to give people a vision for a better future.

I greatly admired the president when he gave his televised Civil Rights speech on the night of June 11, 1963, and aligned himself solidly with the Civil Rights movement. Even then I knew it was a courageous—and dangerous—thing for him to do.

⊕

On November 22, 1963, a few days before Thanksgiving, my high school math teacher, a short man named Mr. Ralph Joseph, walked into my classroom with his head lowered.

"It's official," he announced. "The president has been shot."

I couldn't believe my ears! *John F. Kennedy? Shot?*

FROM MARTIN LUTHER KING JR.'S "WHERE DO WE GO FROM HERE?" SPEECH

Let us be dissatisfied until America will no longer have a high blood pressure of creeds and an anemia of deeds.

Let us be dissatisfied until the tragic walls that separate the outer city of wealth and comfort from the inner city of poverty and despair shall be crushed by the battering rams of the forces of justice.

Let us be dissatisfied until those who live on the outskirts of hope are brought into the metropolis of daily security.

Let us be dissatisfied until slums are cast into the junk heaps of history, and every family will live in a decent, sanitary home.

Let us be dissatisfied until the dark yesterdays of segregated schools will be transformed into bright tomorrows of quality integrated education.

Let us be dissatisfied until integration is not seen as a problem but as an opportunity to participate in the beauty of diversity.

Let us be dissatisfied until men and women, however black they may be, will be judged on the basis of the content of their character, not on the basis of the color of their skin. Let us be dissatisfied.

Let us be dissatisfied until every state capitol will be housed by a governor who will do justly, who will love mercy, and who will walk humbly with his God.

Let us be dissatisfied until from every city hall, justice will roll down like waters, and righteousness like a mighty stream.

Let us be dissatisfied until that day when the lion and the

lamb shall lie down together, and every man will sit under his own vine and fig tree, and none shall be afraid.

Let us be dissatisfied, and men will recognize that out of one blood God made all men to dwell upon the face of the earth.

Let us be dissatisfied until that day when nobody will shout, "White Power!" when nobody will shout, "Black Power!" but everybody will talk about God's power and human power.[4]

Later that day, we received confirmation of the sad news: he was dead.

I was deeply saddened by my president's death. But I guess I wasn't completely surprised. It seemed that whenever someone understood our plight, took a public stand, and made a promise to help us, he signed his death warrant. It had happened to Medgar Evers the past summer, and the list of Civil Rights martyrs was growing. There were some people who would do whatever it took to silence the voices that spoke out against injustice, even if it meant killing people.

I knew my history, and it scared me. But it didn't shock me anymore. In my teenage mind, I was starting to see that it had become the "American way" to kill those who rejected the status quo. For all the fine speeches about equality, the actions of a powerful few spoke much louder.

It came to light later that President Kennedy wasn't surprised by the threat of assassination, either. As the day to fly to Dallas approached, he kept repeating to George Smathers, "God, I hate to go out to Texas. I just hate to go. I have a terrible feeling about going. I wish I could get out of it."[5] But even as he was advised not to make the trip, Kennedy also remarked to his friend Larry Newman, "If this is the way life is, if this is the way it's going to end, this is the way it's going to end."[6]

John F. Kennedy's assassination in Dallas proved yet another heavy, heartbreaking tragedy in my young life. Another dashed hope.

Dr. King later said Kennedy's death was caused "by a

morally inclement climate" that arose from "our constant attempt to cure the cancer of racial injustice with the gasoline of graduation; our readiness to allow arms to be purchased at will and fired at whim."[7]

Those proved terrible, frightening months for our entire country. The United States had just undergone the failed Cuban Bay of Pigs drama, followed by the Cuban Missile Crisis. Questions about Kennedy's death abounded: *Did the Communists kill Kennedy? Did assassin Harvey Lee Oswald act alone? Was JFK's killing the work of a conspiracy? Was the Mafia involved?* Chaos continued to rule in our country when, two days later, nightclub owner Jack Ruby shot and killed Oswald as police led him through the basement of the Dallas jail.

⊕

The president's murder gave my teachers and parents and pastor the perfect opportunity to talk with us children about death and dying, about bombings and hatred. We needed to talk. We needed someone to help clear the air and bring some understanding to the turmoil happening all around us.

But no one talked. Black folk had been conditioned to look the other way when tragedy struck, especially if the victim was one of their own. Whenever my parents talked about bombings or death or sex or politics, they routinely, without fail, asked us children to leave the room.

Mr. Ralph Joseph, my math teacher, explained to my class how presidential succession took place and told us Lyndon

Johnson had become our new president. But he left us on our own to wonder *why* Kennedy was murdered—and on our own to try to find solace in his sudden death.

I don't remember Thanksgiving Day in 1963. I don't remember Christmas that year either. I guess we put up a tree in our living room and decorated it, as we always did. Maybe we had Christmas dinner around our family table. I just can't recall. My heart and mind were numb, and if we celebrated, it was all I could do to go through the motions.

When Mama Lessie was alive, my family would hop in the car on Christmas mornings and drive one hour south to Clanton, where we would celebrate the holidays with my grandparents. They would put a live tree in their front room, and all of us kids would decorate it with paper chains and stars that we'd made at school the week before. My grandmother always cooked turkey and dressing for Christmas dinner. For dessert she made an apple or peach cobbler and sometimes pound cake. We would gather chairs from all over the house and sit around the big dining room table to eat. During the day, Granddaddy would slip out of the house to take money or food to needy people in his church or to check on a sick member.

One Christmas my grandparents bought my brothers a Lionel train set. Mama told us it cost a whole fifty dollars— a lot of money in those days. Granddaddy had helped the boys put it together and play with it. Mama Lessie told me that Granddaddy had always wanted to buy that Lionel train set, but as the father of five daughters, he never got the chance.

Now he had grandsons! Christmas had always brought good memories into my childhood—a bright light shining through the dark days of segregation and Jim Crow laws.

The year of the bombing, Mama Lessie was no longer around, so I know we didn't go to Clanton. It's possible Granddaddy drove up to our home on Christmas Day, but I honestly don't remember. Those carefree Christmases of my childhood seemed like a lifetime ago.

In the years since, I've wondered about that Christmas of 1963 for the families of my four slain friends. The holidays are a time for families to get together, open gifts, and eat food that has been lovingly prepared. Did Denise's family eat Christmas dinner staring at an empty chair at the table? Did Addie's family set up and decorate a Christmas tree? Did Carole's family pay off the dead girl's Christmas gifts in department store layaways? Or did they just decide to leave the gifts there—half-paid and forever unclaimed? And what about the emptiness felt by Cynthia's parents? Both Denise and Cynthia were only children. How in the world did their families survive the holidays without them?

CHAPTER 15

BOMBINGHAM

The deaths of the children followed by the loss of President Kennedy two months later gave birth to a tide of grief and anger—a surge of emotional momentum that helped ensure the passage of the 1964 Civil Rights Act.

U.S. NATIONAL PARK SERVICE[1]

Change does not roll in on the wheels of inevitability, but comes through continuous struggle. And so we must straighten our backs and work for our freedom. A man can't ride you unless your back is bent.

MARTIN LUTHER KING JR.

WHEN 1964 DAWNED, I wondered, *Will the new year bring relief from bombings and some much-needed peace to my city? Will Kennedy's wish of national desegregation ever come true now that he's dead?*

The bombings and killings didn't stop after the calendar page turned. Birmingham's nickname still fit: not much had changed in "Bombingham." With all the mining operations around the area, dynamite was easy to come by and hard to trace. And so was hatred.

Every black family in my neighborhood knew the familiar sound of a bomb exploding. On any given day or night, we'd be in the house or sitting on the front porch and hear the distinctive boom. In an instant, everything would grow still and quiet. We would look at one another and wait for the phone to ring. Within minutes, someone would call us and say, "They just bombed attorney Shores's home [or the Gaston Motel or A. D. King's house or another location]!" We would hang our heads and say a silent prayer.

Spring 1964 came to Birmingham, Alabama, as usual. Turmoil and questions about John F. Kennedy's killer kept the nation in a state of unrest. I was still reeling from the assassination of my president and the deaths of my four friends. I felt miserable and depressed. I couldn't sleep. I thought a lot about death and dying. The cloud still followed me everywhere I went.

At three o'clock one morning in April 1964, we heard an unmistakable boom. The bomb's bright light lit up the sky above our street, and for a few seconds night became day. The force of the blast knocked my brothers Wendell and Kirk out of their top bunk beds with a loud thud. I was asleep in my room and shot up in bed when I heard the shattering glass. *What in the world?* I thought. In my grogginess, it took a moment for me to understand what was going on, but this wasn't the first time something like this had happened. Almost immediately I heard Mrs. Crowell screaming—she was trying to wake up her family and get them out of the house in case another bomb exploded. *I can't believe it's happening again.*

I looked out through the hole where my now-shattered bedroom window had been, and I saw smoke coming from the house across the street. The Crowells' home!

Please, Lord, let the Crowells be alive and unhurt! I jumped out of bed and slipped on my clothes. I had the sinking sensation that sooner or later a bomb would go off that I wouldn't live to talk about. I felt as if it were only a matter of time.

◈

I liked Mrs. Crowell. She was a big woman, about five feet ten and big boned. Her skin was so fair—a sort of reddish yellow—that she almost looked white. Her hair reminded me of actress/singer Diana Ross's, except Diana's was reddish brown. I often wondered whether she was a person of mixed parentage.

Mrs. Crowell was different from the other black women

who lived in my neighborhood. She marched to a different beat. She pulled her long, thick hair back into a ponytail and wore unusual dresses and skirts with colorful printed patterns. She didn't talk like any of us, either. Someone told me, with a smirk, that she was "cultured." An artist by profession, Mrs. Crowell taught music and art. She had traveled the world and collected art from France and Africa. Her house was decorated in a sort of European way—I especially remember all the nude wood statues from Africa she had placed in almost every room.

I spent lots of time at the Crowell home, and I enjoyed being around Mrs. Crowell even though most all the women in our neighborhood kept their distance. I became like a daughter to her. Sometimes we went shopping together, and sometimes she would sit at the beautiful white baby grand piano in her living room and play her heart out. She shared things with me too—recipes, memories from her time abroad, hot dogs cooked on the outside grill. She never fried chicken and cooked greens like my mother did; instead, she collected and made recipes from France. Sometimes white friends of hers came all the way from Paris to eat dinner and spend time with her and her family. She often invited me over to eat with her foreign friends, and I always looked forward to meeting all the interesting guests.

After the explosion, my family and all our neighbors ran out into the street. Mrs. Crowell stood in her front yard in her nightgown, screaming as loud as she could. "My husband and sons are still in the house!" she cried.

Everyone tried to figure out exactly what had happened. It didn't take long. The Klan. A bomb. At first the neighbors stayed in the street, a safe distance from the house. We worried that the Klan might have planted a second, deadlier bomb to explode after a crowd had gathered.

Someone called the Birmingham police. The officers took their time getting there, but they finally arrived. Mr. Crowell and their sons, George and Weymoth, came out the front door, terrified but not hurt. Somehow, inexplicably, they had managed to sleep through the whole thing.

When the situation was assessed, we discovered that the blast had ripped through many of the nearby homes, had broken most of the windows on the neighbors' houses, and had dented cars that were parked on the street. The damage proved great because the homes in my neighborhood sat side by side or faced each other and had simple wooden foundations.

The word around the black community was that the Crowells were bombed because they had too many white people at their house—they needed to be reminded of who they were and the penalty for not obeying the rules. I guess the Klan wanted to teach the Crowells a lesson about mixing and socializing with whites.

When the sun came up that morning, the Crowells packed up their belongings and furniture and moved out of the damaged house. They never came back. They fully intended to leave this memory behind.

Later that morning, about an hour before lunchtime,

Alabama governor George Wallace himself came to our neighborhood. Several security cars accompanied him—for protection, I reckon. I recognized him from the television news, the newspapers, and the *Time* magazine cover the past September.

Why is he here? I asked myself. With some pomp and circumstance, Wallace stood in front of the Crowell house and gave a brief speech to the crowd of black spectators, white reporters, photographers, and our neighbors.

"I apologize for this bombing," I remember hearing him telling us. He said something about it being "a horrible act." He promised, "We are going to get the perpetrators!" I think I recall his asking, "Is everybody okay?"

I felt confused. *Why would Governor Wallace come to our neighborhood?* I wondered. *It's obvious he doesn't like us!*

As I listened to him speak and strive to show some sense of sympathy, I couldn't help but remember his famous inaugural words the year before: "Segregation today! Segregation tomorrow! Segregation forever!"

Surely that speech then made a more permanent impression on my young mind than his offer of apology now.

Did Wallace ever get the perpetrators, as he promised? No. This bombing turned out to be just one more "unsolved" explosion in Bombingham, Alabama.

Not long after the Crowell house bombing, another close neighbor, Mrs. Ryles, came home from teaching school one day and saw a mysterious brown paper bag lying in the bushes by her front porch. She bent down and tried to examine it.

She thought it looked suspicious, so she called the police. They came, checked it out, and found fifteen sticks of dynamite in the bag.

⊕

Kirk, Wendell, and I had now experienced two bombings—two close calls in our lives. After the church bombing in September 1963, Kirk stopped speaking, except when he felt it absolutely necessary. The next April, after he and Wendell had been thrown from their beds, Kirk became even more withdrawn. What was going through his young mind? We never discussed it.

When Birmingham's Phillips High School finally integrated in 1963, my brother Kirk enrolled as one of the school's first black students. Although we never explicitly talked about it, I imagine this must have been a difficult experience for him, especially with his quiet nature. He was smart in math but came home with a C on his report card in math that year, so my mother went to school and asked the teacher about it. She was told that Kirk had sat in the wrong seat and was given the wrong grade by mistake. That experience seemed to diminish his faith in people, and he became even more quiet and withdrawn after that.

After school Kirk worked part-time at Birmingham's Greyhound bus station. "I've never seen a person so quiet," his employer once told my mother. "He just works. He never says a thing!"

Kirk eventually earned an MBA from Auburn University, became a seasoned chess player, a vegetarian, and a marathon runner. He never married. He never fathered children. He worked for the Department of Transportation in Atlanta, Georgia, for two decades. A devout Christian, he tried his best to follow God's teachings all his life. My inclination is that he forgave the people who had wronged him, but I don't know for sure. We never discussed it. My silent little brother, Kirk, died in November 2000.

⊕

During those weeks and months after the bombing, I kept on helping Pastor Cross while we waited for workers to complete the Sixteenth Street Baptist Church renovations. The pastor asked me to plan a church program based on Psalm 23. I had read this psalm of David's many times, but now when I read it, the words spoke directly to my heart and brought me some comfort.

> The LORD is my shepherd, I shall not be in want.
> He makes me lie down in green pastures,
>   he leads me beside quiet waters,
> he restores my soul.
>   He guides me in paths of righteousness
>   for his name's sake.
> Even though I walk
>   through the valley of the shadow of death,

I will fear no evil,
   for you are with me;
   your rod and your staff,
   they comfort me.
You prepare a table before me
   in the presence of my enemies.
   You anoint my head with oil;
   my cup overflows.
Surely goodness and love will follow me
   all the days of my life,
   and I will dwell in the house of the LORD
   forever.

I found David's psalm to be a great source of strength. I read it every night before I dressed for bed, and eventually I memorized it. But I still had questions and uncertainties about life and death.

Even though I walk through the valley of the shadow of death? Death proved to be no shadow in my life—it was real. And I walked near that valley every day!

Eventually another family bought the house, fixed it up, and lived there for many years. Still, even years later, no one spoke about the Crowell house bombing. As a black community, we tried hard to forget it. But there was no denying its shadow over our neighborhood.

CHAPTER 16

WILL THE VIOLENCE EVER END?

*The Negro baby born in America today, regardless of the section of
the nation in which he is born, has about one-half as much chance of
completing high school as a white baby born in the same place on the
same day; one third as much chance of completing college; one third as
much chance of becoming a professional man; twice as much chance
of becoming unemployed; about one-seventh as much chance of earning
$10,000 a year; a life expectancy which is seven years shorter; and the
prospects of earning only half as much.*

JOHN F. KENNEDY, JUNE 11, 1963[1]

RACIAL VIOLENCE, BOMBINGS, AND MURDERS continued during the summer of 1964. *When will the violence stop?* I asked myself again and again. I became physically sick to my stomach when I heard about three more Civil Rights workers killed in Mississippi.

Michael Schwerner and Andrew Goodman were two white men who worked with CORE (Congress of Racial Equality), a group that encouraged black Americans to register to vote and coached them on how to pass the voter registration exam. Along with James Chaney, an African-American from Mississippi, they were heading south to Mississippi to investigate the burning of a church there. On Sunday night, June 21, 1964, the three men disappeared. We watched the news report on television, and that night I overheard my mother talking with a neighbor on our front porch about the missing men.

"I wonder where they are," my mother said. She was especially concerned because she had four sons of her own. When we found out two of the men were white, it struck terror in our hearts. It seemed Civil Rights workers' lives were worthless—black or white—when they stood up for black people.

The next day we heard that someone had found a burned-out station wagon in the Bogue Chitto swamp. A month and a half later, the FBI discovered the three men's bodies buried in a fifteen-feet-deep earthen dam. Three years later, on February 27, 1967, the Neshoba County deputy sheriff and eighteen others (all Ku Klux Klan members) were indicted for the murders. A two-week federal trial in Meridian, Mississippi, resulted in seven guilty verdicts and sentences ranging from three to ten years.[2]

Good-hearted people paid a dear price for standing up for African-Americans' equal rights. Before his untimely death, President John F. Kennedy had promised my people he would set the wheels in motion to outlaw segregation in businesses such as theaters, restaurants, and hotels and in public places such as swimming pools, libraries, and other public facilities. He also promised to ban discrimination in employment. Technically, according to the 1954 *Brown v. Board of Education* decision, the law called for the desegregation of all-white public schools as well. But as late as 1963, only twelve thousand of the 3 million African-Americans in the South attended integrated schools.[3]

That summer, on July 2, 1964, President Lyndon B. Johnson signed the Civil Rights Act of 1964, which outlawed segregation in the workplace, in schools, and in public places. But this measure was not without opposition. Johnson's main opponent was his longtime friend and mentor Richard B. Russell, who told the Senate, "We will resist to the bitter end any measure or any movement which would have a tendency to bring about social equality and intermingling and amalgamation of the races in our [Southern] states." Russell then organized eighteen Southern Democratic senators in filibustering this bill.[4] I thought, *This man must be a friend of George Wallace. Surely not all white men think this way!*

A week before the Civil Rights bill became law, *Newsweek* magazine published a nationwide poll titled "The Negro Revolution—U.S. Attitudes Now." Most of the nation said they believed it was wrong for unions and churches to refuse black people membership and for employers to refuse to hire African-Americans. Less than half, however, believed it was wrong for neighborhoods to refuse to rent or sell homes to black people or for social clubs to refuse to admit them. More than half of the nation thought black people wanted to take over white jobs. But less than half believed black people wanted to move into white neighborhoods, take over politics, and enroll in white schools. Only 23 percent of Americans believed black people wanted to marry and/or have sexual relations with whites.[5] Clearly, we still had a long way to go.

It was only two years earlier, in January of 1962, that Birmingham's Bull Connor had refused to desegregate the city's public facilities. He chose the extreme of closing down the city's sixty-eight parks, thirty-eight playgrounds, six swimming pools, and four golf courses rather than allowing black people to enjoy them.[6]

"Federal meddling," Connor had remarked. Along with the other two city commissioners, Jabo Waggoner and Art Hanes, Connor bought concrete and poured it in the golf course holes.

Things were changing in the South. But slowly.

◈

That autumn, on October 14, 1964, I heard that Dr. Martin Luther King Jr. had been awarded the Nobel Peace Prize for advocating a policy of nonviolence.

Surely he deserves it, I thought.

King traveled to Oslo, Norway, and on December 10, 1964, delivered his acceptance speech. I had always loved and admired Dr. King, and when I read his speech, that love and admiration deepened.

"I accept the Nobel Prize for Peace," Dr. King said, "at a moment when 22 million Negroes of the United States of America are engaged in a creative battle to end the long night of racial injustice. I accept this award on behalf of a Civil Rights movement which is moving with determination and a majestic scorn for risk and danger to establish a reign of freedom and a rule of justice."

He continued, "I am mindful that only yesterday in Birmingham, Alabama, our children, crying out for brotherhood, were answered with fire hoses, snarling dogs and even death. I am mindful that only yesterday in Philadelphia, Mississippi, young people seeking to secure the right to vote were brutalized and murdered. And only yesterday more than 40 houses of worship in the State of Mississippi alone were bombed or burned because they offered a sanctuary to those who would not accept segregation. I am mindful that debilitating and grinding poverty afflicts my people and chains them to the lowest rung of the economic ladder."

Dr. King ended his speech with both a question and a statement: "Therefore, I must ask why this prize is awarded to a movement which is beleaguered and committed to unrelenting struggle; to a movement which has not won the very peace and brotherhood which is the essence of the Nobel Prize. . . . Most of these people will never make the

FROM MARTIN LUTHER KING JR.'S
NOBEL PEACE PRIZE ACCEPTANCE SPEECH

This evening I would like to use this lofty and historic platform to discuss what appears to me to be the most pressing problem confronting mankind today. Modern man has brought this whole world to an awe-inspiring threshold of the future. He has reached new and astonishing peaks of scientific success. He has produced machines that think and instruments that peer into the unfathomable ranges of interstellar space. He has built gigantic bridges to span the seas and gargantuan buildings to kiss the skies. His airplanes and spaceships have dwarfed distance, placed time in chains, and carved highways through the stratosphere. This is a dazzling picture of modern man's scientific and technological progress.

Yet, in spite of these spectacular strides in science and technology, and still unlimited ones to come, something basic is missing. There is a sort of poverty of the spirit which stands in glaring contrast to our scientific and technological abundance. The richer we have become materially, the poorer we have become morally and spiritually. We have learned to fly the air like birds and swim the sea like fish, but we have not learned the simple art of living together as brothers. . . .

This call for a worldwide fellowship that lifts neighborly concern beyond one's tribe, race, class, and nation is in reality a call for an all-embracing and unconditional love for all men. This oft misunderstood and misinterpreted concept so readily dismissed by the Nietzsches of the world as a weak and cowardly force has now become an absolute necessity for the survival of man. When I speak of love I am not speaking of some sentimental and weak response which is little more than emotional bosh. I am speaking of that force which all of the great religions have seen as the supreme unifying principle of life. Love is somehow the key that unlocks the door which leads to ultimate reality. . . .

We can no longer afford to worship the God of hate or bow before the altar of retaliation. The oceans of history are made turbulent by the ever-rising tides of hate. History is cluttered with the wreckage of nations and individuals that pursued this self-defeating path of hate. Love is the key to the solution of the problems of the world.

Let me close by saying that I have the personal faith that mankind will somehow rise up to the occasion and give new directions to an age drifting rapidly to its doom. In spite of the tensions and uncertainties of this period something profoundly meaningful is taking place. Old systems of exploitation and oppression are passing away, and out of the womb of a frail world new systems of justice and equality are being born. . . . "The people who sat in darkness have seen a great light." Here and there an individual or group dares to love, and rises to the majestic heights of moral maturity. So in a real sense this is a great time to be alive. Therefore, I am not yet discouraged about the future. Granted that the easygoing optimism of yesterday is impossible. Granted that those who pioneer in the struggle for peace and freedom will still face uncomfortable jail terms, painful threats of death; they will still be battered by the storms of persecution, leading them to the nagging feeling that they can no longer bear such a heavy burden, and the temptation of wanting to retreat to a more quiet and serene life. Granted that we face a world crisis which leaves us standing so often amid the surging murmur of life's restless sea. But every crisis has both its dangers and its opportunities. It can spell either salvation or doom. In a dark confused world the kingdom of God may yet reign in the hearts of men.[7]

headlines and their names will not appear in *Who's Who*. Yet when years have rolled past and when the blazing light of truth is focused on this marvelous age in which we live—men and women will know and children will be taught that we have a finer land, a better people, a more noble civilization—because these humble children of God were willing to suffer for righteousness' sake."[8]

These humble children of God were willing to suffer for righteousness' sake, I repeated to myself over and over. When Dr. King said those words, I thought of all those courageous souls who had died to help make Dr. King's dream come true for my people—Cynthia, Carole, Denise, Addie, John F. Kennedy, Schwerner, Goodman, Chaney, and many others throughout the ages. Other names would soon join the list of martyrs: Jimmy Lee Jackson, an impoverished, black, twenty-six-year-old advocate of equal voting rights, killed on February 18, 1965, by an Alabama state trooper during a small protest in Marion, Alabama; James Reeb, a white Unitarian minister from Boston, who on Dr. King's invitation traveled to Selma, Alabama, and was beaten to death by a mob of white men in March 1965; and others. I wondered about the safety of Reverend Fred Shuttlesworth, the fearless Civil Rights advocate and the pastor of Birmingham's Bethel Baptist Church. Would he, too, become a martyr? And I worried about Dr. Martin Luther King Jr. himself.

Perhaps it's only a matter of time before someone kills Dr. King, too, I thought.

On August 6, 1965, President Johnson signed the Voting

Rights Act, ending the practice of requiring literacy, knowledge, or character tests (administered solely to African-
Americans) to keep them from registering to vote. Within a
year, 450,000 Southern blacks successfully registered to vote
for the first time.[9]

⊕

In the fall of 1965, I left Birmingham and traveled to
Nashville, Tennessee, to go to college. Rather than fight possible racial roadblocks, I enrolled at all-black Fisk University,
as my parents had suggested. I enjoyed my classes and my
professors. But I found it difficult to study and concentrate
like I once had. Ever since the church bombing, I had lost
my enthusiasm for school.

The gloom and depression that constantly tormented my
soul deepened. I wanted to be alone. I attended few social gath-
erings and made few friends. Sleep was one of the few things
that helped me escape the world, and I tried to sleep a lot. But
deep sleep continued to elude me and was proving to have been
a prebombing gift. I often sat under an isolated tree on a distant
part of campus and wrote in my journal. Writing seemed to
help me make some sense out of life. But my written ponderings
came from a dark, depressed heart. I wrote of pain and suffering
and death. I saved those writings—they now sit in a box on a
closet shelf—and to this day it still hurts me to read them. I've
never shared them with anyone, not even my husband.

During those college years, I discovered that a glass or

two of wine took the edge off my inner pain and helped me forget. I shared my deep pain with no one but God. Few of my classmates or professors knew of my church-bombing experience or any of the other traumatic events from my childhood. I just didn't talk about any of it. Drink would eventually become my friend, my artificial comforter. I never would have imagined where this drinking would lead. I was too wrapped up in finding a way to ease the pain and depression—in making myself feel happy, at least for a while. It would take me a long time to realize that the relief a drink brought was always temporary and that the pain and depression always returned. It was not a permanent fix.

I wasn't sure if my open and bleeding wound would ever heal.

One day I was feeling overwhelmed by the torment I felt. I didn't know what to do with the sense of hopelessness and despair that plagued me. So I scribbled this letter to God, imagining I was having a conversation with him:

"God, why didn't you take me too? Why did you leave me here?"

"Carolyn," I sensed God saying to me, "I needed Cynthia, Addie, Denise, and Carole to come. I needed you to stay."

"But I don't want to stay," I pleaded. "I want to come too."

"Carolyn, I still have something special for you to do. I need you to tell this story."

"But I miss Cynthia so much. Could you just make the pain go away? It hurts to wake up in the morning, and I am so afraid."

"I know you miss her, Carolyn. But she is just fine. Carolyn, don't cry. And don't be afraid. I love you, and I am always with you."

"Will you let Cynthia know that I paid for her cap and shirt? I gave them both to her mom. And tell her I miss her and I'm sorry I didn't get to say good-bye."

"Carolyn, she is happy. She is fine. And you will see her and the other girls again. They will be waiting."

And then I sensed God planting in me a vision for my future. "Carolyn, I need you to tell people that this is not about skin color or ethnicity or religion. It is about love, it is about forgiveness, it is about reconciliation. I need you to be my messenger, my ambassador. They will know I allowed you to live—I saved you so you could bear personal witness to my power to restore and forgive and draw people to me. Just lift me up."

"Lift Him Up"—one of my very favorite hymns that we always sang at Granddaddy's church. I got the message. God was showing me what he wanted me to do.

"Tell them about me. Tell them about Cynthia, Addie, Denise, and Carole. Tell them that when they are reconciled to me, they can be reconciled to each other."

I wasn't there yet, but I thanked God for holding me gently in his arms until I could find my way.

⊕

While at Fisk, I continued to drink to numb my inner pain, and gradually I began to need drinks of increasing strength.

I began to look forward to my times alone to get my fix. My journal entries grew darker and more disturbing. I seemed to be on the periphery of life, not really a part of it. I felt as though I didn't belong anywhere, as though I lived separated from life by a glass window. I stood on the outside of that window and looked in, not really part of anything.

"This is a time in American history," I wrote one day, "when people say nothing. People are murdered, and no one says, 'This is wrong' or does anything about it."

God gave me one unique gift during this time—my friend Mary Kate Bush. Mary Kate was also from Birmingham. I first met her when she and I had entered the Gaston spelling bee in the seventh grade. Like me, Mary Kate had suffered many wounds. She knew when I needed to be alone, and I knew when she needed to be alone. But when I needed to talk or cry, Mary Kate was always there to listen. The lives we had lived already, at such a young and tender age, gave way to many discussions about the future and what it held for us. Sometimes, it was hard to believe that the future held anything except more pain. It was providential that we would live together for those four years at college, and after graduation, we continued a friendship that was a healing balm. Through Mary Kate, God enabled me to understand true spiritual friendship. He blessed me with a "forever friend," one who would always be there for me.

CHAPTER 17

THE DEATHS OF THE DREAMERS

◈

You see things, and you say "why?" But I dream things that never were,
and I say "why not?"

GEORGE BERNARD SHAW, *BACK TO METHUSELAH*

The ultimate measure of a man is not where he stands in moments
of comfort and convenience, but where he stands at times of challenge
and controversy.

MARTIN LUTHER KING JR.

IN THE FALL OF 1982, Geraldine Watts Bell wrote an article in *Down Home* magazine (a new publication started by Denise's father, Chris McNair) about the glaring absence of a memorial in Birmingham for the girls who had died in the church bombing.

Bell wrote, "The time is long overdue for Birmingham citizens to establish a perpetual commemoration in honor of the sacrifices made by these [girls'] families. Although there are several memorials to the deaths of these young people in other states, there has been no significant effort on the part of Birmingham and Alabama citizenry to remember these sacrifices appropriately."

She continued, "It can be readily seen, then, that there is an urgent need for the citizens of Birmingham and the State of Alabama to seek some type of appropriate commemoration for this tragic act. . . . This one act awakened the conscience of the nation to the fact that something was not right in the way Black citizens are treated."[1]

Several decades have passed. We're still waiting.

⊕

By the late 1960s, a few things had changed in the South, thanks to some key leaders. Former all-white public schools had opened their doors to black students, as had department stores, restaurants, lunch counters, swimming pools, libraries, and other private and tax-supported facilities. African-Americans could now register to vote without undergoing ridiculous qualification games, taking difficult exams, experiencing Klan intimidation, and paying "blacks only" poll taxes.

But while visible changes had taken place, I noticed that the invisible changes came much more slowly.

We can, by law, change the outside, I thought. *But we can't so easily change people's hearts. How do we change the inside?*

⊕

On the night of April 4, 1968, I was studying in my dorm room at Fisk. Some fellow students ran through the halls and pounded on my door.

"Carolyn!" they screamed. "Dr. King's been murdered in Memphis!"

"Dr. Martin Luther King?" I asked. "Are you sure?" I felt like someone had punched me in the heart. *Surely not! Not Dr. King!*

"Yes, Carolyn! Dr. King! And riots are happening everywhere—all over the entire country!" they shouted as they ran down the hall and pounded on more dorm doors. "Who knows what might happen before the night is over!"

A frightening thought entered my mind: *Racial war! It's really happening! We're all going to die because of this!*

The other female students and I ran from our rooms and into the hall. We squatted on the floor with our backs pressed firmly against the wall, our knees pulled up to our chests, our heads lowered and protected by our crossed arms. We had practiced Fisk's security drill many times. My whole body trembled. Students cried. We all feared the worst.

Minutes became hours. We sat in silence for a long time. Each of us had plenty of time to think and pray.

Here we go again, I thought. *Why did I think racial problems here in Nashville would be any different from racial problems back in Birmingham? Maybe there is no escaping it. Ever.*

That night I sat in the hallway in fear and thought about Dr. King. I remembered the many times I'd heard him speak from the pulpit of Sixteenth Street Baptist Church. He worked so hard to open up the doors that had been closed for so long to African-Americans. I recalled his leadership as we marched down the streets of Birmingham that May in 1963, when the pressure from the firefighters' water hose had torn off part of my hair. I thought about Dr. King's courage, his dedication to us, and his struggle for freedom. As I remembered him, I hummed some of the songs he'd encouraged us to sing during the days when so many of us had met in the church sanctuary and then marched down the streets of Birmingham:

Oh freedom!
Oh freedom!
Oh freedom over me
And before I'll be a slave
I'll be buried in my grave.
And go home to my Lord and be free.

As I softly sang the song, I thought, *Dr. King is free now. They cannot bother him anymore.*

Then I remembered something I'd heard at one of the rallies: *Didn't Reverend Shuttlesworth tell us that people might have to die in order to gain that freedom?*

"And before I'll be a slave I'll be buried in my grave. And go home to my Lord and be free."

At that moment I understood why Dr. King had encouraged us to sing. Surely the songs helped us understand that death may be necessary. Perhaps they gave us some kind of resolve as we sang them—and also the courage to face our own death someday, if that's what was necessary for freedom.

I feared what might happen outside my dorm walls later that night, and I started to sing the song that had always given me strength in the midst of great fear:

All along this Christian journey,
I want Jesus to walk with me.
I want Jesus to walk with me.
All along this Christian journey,
I want Jesus to walk with me.
In my troubles, walk with me.
When I'm dying, walk with me.
All along this Christian journey,
I want Jesus to walk with me.
I want Jesus to walk with me.

That night, with my back pressed against the hard wall of my dorm hallway, I thought about the pain Dr. King must have felt when he heard that Sixteenth Street Baptist Church had been bombed and that four girls had died. People told me Dr. King's eulogy for my slain friends had brought deep comfort to the girls' families. I remembered how Dr. King had grieved that November 1963 when he learned President Kennedy had been shot and killed. Now Dr. King himself had been assassinated. I was devastated.

Dr. King, I cried out silently, *I feel like I have lost a member of my own family.*

I thought about a quote I'd heard by Dr. Cornell West, a professor at Princeton: "You cannot lead the people if you don't love the people. And you can't save the people if you're not willing to serve the people." Dr. King had been willing to do both.

"I wonder what's happening outside." My thoughts were interrupted by a fellow student who sat beside me in the hallway.

"I don't know," I whispered back. "The school officials told us to stay here in lockdown."

Student leaders came to every dormitory and told us whatever messages they had been given—we didn't have a PA system or a loudspeaker. "Do not go out of the building!" they warned us. "People are shooting each other out there!"

Shooting each other?

I thought about my mother, father, sister, and brothers.

Are they okay? Are they safe? The one pay phone at the end of the hall wasn't working, so I had no way to telephone them. During that long, tense night, back in my room, I lay still and quiet as my thoughts took me back to all the pain and horror and tragedy I had tried so hard to put behind me.

I thought, *A drink could blot out all the ugly and painful things around me.*

As I waited, another terrifying thought came to mind: *What will happen now that Dr. King is dead?*

Dr. King, I whispered, *who will help us keep striving for your dream—our dream—of Birmingham's black and white children walking hand in hand?*

The next day I learned the tragic facts about Dr. King's death. He had traveled to Memphis, Tennessee, to support black sanitation workers who were being treated unfairly in their jobs. It was here that he made his famous "I've Been to the Mountaintop" speech. After his speech the previous evening, April 4, he returned to his room at the Lorraine Motel on Mulberry Street to dress for dinner. He was running a little late. Ralph Abernathy, Jesse Jackson, and other Civil Rights leaders were waiting outside for him.

When Dr. King stepped out of his room, a white man— a petty criminal named James Earl Ray—shot him. The bullet entered King's right jaw, traveled through his neck, severed his spinal cord, and stopped in his shoulder blade. He fell to the balcony floor. His friends rushed him to St. Joseph's Hospital. He died at 7:05 that night.[3]

Ray had fired the fatal shot from the bathroom of a nearby

FROM MARTIN LUTHER KING JR.'S "I'VE BEEN TO THE MOUNTAINTOP" SPEECH

Something is happening in our world. The masses of people are rising up. And wherever they are assembled today, whether they are in Johannesburg, South Africa; Nairobi, Kenya; Accra, Ghana; New York City; Atlanta, Georgia; Jackson, Mississippi; or Memphis, Tennessee—the cry is always the same: "We want to be free." . . .

We aren't going to let any mace stop us. We are masters in our nonviolent movement in disarming police forces; they don't know what to do. I've seen them so often. I remember in Birmingham, Alabama, when we were in that majestic struggle there, we would move out of the Sixteenth Street Baptist Church day after day; by the hundreds we would move out. And Bull Connor would tell them to send the dogs forth, and they did come; but we just went before the dogs singing, "Ain't gonna let nobody turn me around."

Bull Connor next would say, "Turn the fire hoses on." And as I said to you the other night, Bull Connor didn't know history. He knew a kind of physics that somehow didn't relate to the transphysics that we knew about. And that was the fact that there was a certain kind of fire that no water could put out. And we went before the fire hoses; we had known water. If we were Baptist or some other denominations, we had been immersed. If we were Methodist, and some others, we had been sprinkled, but we knew water. That couldn't stop us.

And we just went on before the dogs and we would look at them; and we'd go on before the water hoses and we would look at it, and we'd just go on singing, "Over my head I see freedom in the air." And then we would be thrown in the paddy wagons, and sometimes we were stacked in there like sardines in a can. And they would throw us in, and old Bull would say, "Take 'em off," and they did; and we would just go in the paddy wagon singing, "We Shall Overcome." And every now and then we'd get in jail, and we'd see the jailers looking through the windows being moved by our prayers, and being moved by our words and our songs. And there was a power there which Bull Connor couldn't adjust to; and so we ended up transforming Bull into a steer, and we won our struggle in Birmingham. . . .

We've got some difficult days ahead. But it really doesn't matter with me now, because I've been to the mountaintop.

And I don't mind.

Like anybody, I would like to live a long life. Longevity has its place. But I'm not concerned about that now. I just want to do God's will. And he's allowed me to go up to the mountain. And I've looked over. And I've seen the Promised Land. I may not get there with you. But I want you to know tonight, that we, as a people, will get to the promised land!

And so I'm happy, tonight.

I'm not worried about anything.

I'm not fearing any man!

Mine eyes have seen the glory of the coming of the Lord![2]

rooming house. Witnesses said that moments after the shoot-ing, they saw Ray run from the building carrying a bundle (his gun).

Oh, the pain he must have suffered, I thought when I heard how Dr. King had died.

Dr. King's murder caused immediate riots in more than one hundred cities across the United States. Four thousand members of the National Guard landed in Memphis to help manage the angry, grief-stricken crowds. Officials ordered a dusk-to-dawn curfew to maintain order.[4] The entire nation was reeling.

British police finally located Ray at London's Heathrow Airport on June 8, 1968, and arrested him. Ray put his head in his hands and cried when they cuffed him. Investigators found Ray's fingerprints on the rifle, scope, and binoculars. He pleaded guilty at his trial the following March. The judge sentenced him to ninety-nine years in prison.

After the sentencing, however, Ray recanted his guilty plea. He named who he claimed was the real shooter—a man he called "Raoul." He suggested a conspiracy and government cover-up.

In 1997 Dr. King's son Dexter visited James Earl Ray in prison. Ray convinced Dexter he was innocent, and the King family agreed with Dexter. A retrial was requested, but Ray, seventy, died of liver failure on April 23, 1998, before the new trial could take place.[5]

After King's assassination, I worried that the Civil Rights dream might end. But over the next few years, I saw how firmly Dr. King had planted the vision in people's hearts, inspiring both black and white Americans to take up the torch and continue the fight for equal rights. King's life ended, but his dream of freedom lived on.

⊕

On June 5, 1968, just sixty-two days after Dr. King's murder, Robert F. Kennedy was shot in Los Angeles. He died twenty-six hours later. I could hardly believe the tragic news.

How many more people must die? I asked myself.

I had admired and appreciated Bobby Kennedy. Like his brother John and Dr. King, Bobby had reached out to the poor and disenfranchised—especially inner-city, impoverished blacks. As attorney general and later as a senator, he had supported racial and educational equality—and asked the American people to do the same. The night Bobby Kennedy died, he had just won the California Democratic primary, which meant he had a strong chance to win the party's presidential nomination. But as with his brother, Bobby's time was cut short. "Each time a man stands up for an ideal or acts to improve the lot of others or strikes out against injustice, he sends forth a tiny ripple of hope," RFK had said. "And crossing each other from a million different centers of energy and daring, those ripples build a current that can sweep down the mightiest walls of oppression and resistance."[6]

As U.S. attorney general (January 1960 to September 1964), Robert Kennedy had actively enforced Civil Rights laws and was deeply committed to African-Americans' equal right to vote. On May 6, 1961, he had traveled to the University of Georgia to deliver one of his first major talks as attorney general. In that speech, RFK compared the domestic struggle for Civil Rights to the free world's fight against communism. In 1962 he had sent U.S. marshals to Oxford, Mississippi, to enforce James Meredith's enrollment into the University of Mississippi.

In 1967, at the invitation of Dr. Marian Wright Edelman, Bobby Kennedy had visited the poor shantytowns in the Mississippi Delta and saw personally the plight of the poor in that area. Kennedy visited one poor family with many children and no heat. Trying to make conversation with a small boy, Kennedy asked him, "What did you have for lunch today?"

"Haven't had lunch," the boy replied.

Kennedy looked at his watch. "It's three o'clock in the afternoon and you haven't had lunch yet?"

"No," the boy said. "Sometimes we eat just one time a day."

After that visit, Kennedy returned to the White House determined to change conditions in the Mississippi Delta and other impoverished parts of the South.

Now he, too, was dead.

Within the span of a decade, I had watched my beloved grandmother die in the basement of Princeton Hospital, I had survived two bombings, I had seen four friends murdered, and I had lost three compassionate leaders to assassins' bullets: John F. Kennedy, Dr. Martin Luther King Jr., and Robert F. Kennedy.

And I had not yet turned twenty-one years old.

CHAPTER 18

JE-ROMEO

⊕

Faith is taking the first step even when you don't see the whole staircase.

MARTIN LUTHER KING JR.

We know not what we should pray for as we ought . . . [but] we know that all things work together for good to them that love God, to them who are the called according to his purpose.

ROMANS 8:26, 28, KJV

DURING MY DARKEST DAYS at Fisk University, God sent Jerome to me. At first, I didn't realize Jerome was God's gift. I prayed each day that God would take away the pain and the depression, the dark cloud. God heard my prayer, but he answered it in a way I never could have imagined. He sent me Jerome, that I might see a reflection of God's love. Jerome loved me unconditionally, like God loved me. It was true then. It is still true today.

During my freshman year at Fisk, in 1965, a friend introduced us. "Carolyn, I want you to meet one of my homeboys. His name is Jerome."

I noticed the tall, slender, good-looking young man. Jerome looked at me and smiled. "My name's really Je-*Romeo!*" he said.

Je-Romeo? I thought. *This guy's really stuck on himself. He thinks he's something really special. Sorry, Je-Romeo! Not interested!*

"Hello, Jerome," I said and walked away.

The next time I saw Jerome, I was standing in Fisk's cafeteria line. I was hungry, and the line in front of me stretched a long way.

"Hello, homegirl!" He walked toward me and eased into the lunch line beside me.

My, my, I thought. *If it's not that stuck-up Je-Romeo! He so smoothly broke into the cafeteria line, and nobody objected. Amazing.*

We filled our trays with food and ate lunch at the same table. *No big deal,* I thought.

The next time I saw Jerome, he was in my dorm building.

As part of my on-campus job, I worked behind the desk on the first floor and greeted dorm guests. He asked me to page another girl in the dorm. When I turned away to pick up the loudspeaker to call her, he said, "Hey! You look good in those jeans. Can we go on a date?"

For some reason, I agreed. I learned that Jerome grew up in Aliceville, Alabama, where his mother taught school. His father worked at the Fairfield Works, a steel mill in Birmingham. His parents had a strong marriage even though they lived a "commuter marriage."

Jerome was two years ahead of me at Fisk. We began attending campus dances together, and before long we became a steady twosome. Jerome was a good dancer and a fun date. We fell in love and were married on January 30, 1968.

Jerome knew little about me when we got married. He knew I belonged to Sixteenth Street Baptist Church in Birmingham, but I didn't tell him I had witnessed the 1963 bombing and the deaths of my friends. He never questioned my inner sadness or my desire to be alone.

Jerome graduated from Fisk and was drafted into the Air Force. He was stationed at Robbins Air Force Base in Valdosta, Georgia, while I continued my education at Fisk in Nashville. We visited each other as often as we could.

After about a year of marriage, I became pregnant with our first child. After I graduated, my mother and father encouraged me to come home to Birmingham and live with them until the baby was born. My daughter, Leigh, arrived on September 26, 1969—my mother's birthday.

Leigh was four months old when the Air Force sent Jerome to Korea, and during the thirteen months he was gone, I continued to live with my parents. When Jerome returned from overseas, we moved to Orlando, Florida. He took a management job with Sears. On July 12, 1973, I delivered our second daughter, Joya.

Life was good. I had a husband I deeply loved and two beautiful, healthy girls. God had blessed me tremendously. But I still couldn't shake the depression. The sadness weighed heavily on my heart. Jerome didn't understand it.

"Carolyn," he often asked me, "what's wrong?"

I don't know why he always asked that question. I thought I was doing a good job keeping the pain buried inside, but apparently some things showed more than I realized.

"Nothing," I'd always answer. I never told him the reason because I really had no idea where the sadness and depression came from.

My drinking increased during our two years in Orlando. Jerome knew I had a small glass of wine on occasion. But he had no idea the immense volume of alcohol I consumed on a daily basis. During the days, after Jerome left for work, I drank vodka—mostly because Jerome couldn't smell it on my breath when he came home. I had big bottles of vodka and gin hidden all over the house. I could easily drink half a bottle a day. I hid the liquor inside my shoes in the bedroom closet, in the bathroom dirty clothes hamper, in the laundry room, and in other secret places.

The more I drank, the colder I became to Jerome. I treated

him with indifference, and I stayed aloof and emotionally distant. I was afraid to share my feelings with him—I didn't really understand these bleak emotions myself. I guess I just thought this was life—that some people are born happy and some aren't. I didn't know how to get past it. But Jerome quietly accepted my isolating behavior.

As a youth, I had loved people and parties. But now my life seemed so uncertain. I was frightened. I got scared when Jerome traveled out of town and I had to stay by myself. So many unanswered questions were spinning around in my mind. *What was happening to me? Why had I changed so much?*

Loud noises also terrified me. I flew into a panic every time a truck backfired or a balloon popped at a child's birthday party. And, as hard as I tried, I still couldn't sleep well at night.

Even now, I had not connected the Sixteenth Street Church bombing and my friends' deaths with my depresssion. All I knew was that I was miserable. I hated life, and I had no idea why.

One day in 1973, Jerome came home from work with news. "Carolyn, Sears wants to transfer me to Atlanta, Georgia."

We packed our belongings and moved. But things proved no better for me in Atlanta than they'd been in Orlando. I stayed home during the long days and cared for my daughters. I continued to drink vodka and gin, hiding the bottles in secret places all over the house. I grew even more despondent. I didn't want to live anymore. I thought about death a lot, and I didn't know why. I didn't think there was any-thing unusual about a constant preoccupation with death. My life was like an open, bleeding wound that had festered and would not heal.

I felt totally alone. *I have no one to help me*, I thought. *Maybe I should just die and be done with all this.*

When Jerome left for work one morning, I fed and dressed my children and then poured myself an orange juice with vodka. One drink followed another.

As the girls played outside, I watched television and nursed my drinks. During the commercial break, the station gave a number for the suicide hotline.

"Are you confused about life? Don't know which way to turn? Need someone to talk to?" the ad asked. Then the narrator added, "Call this number. Counselors are waiting to take your call." A phone number flashed across the TV screen.

We had been in Atlanta about a year, and I had not made any friends. I wanted to talk to someone besides my children. I was sad and lonely, but I still hadn't thought through what was causing it. Even as I dialed the number on the screen, I'm not sure I realized how down I was—I just wanted someone to talk to.

A counselor answered, and I gave my first name only. I explained that I was new to Atlanta and that I was feel-ing sad and lonely and a bit overwhelmed. And that I just needed to talk. It had been ten years since the bombing, but I still thought about that awful day or the girls—usually

Cynthia—daily. I had been back to Birmingham many times since then, but I'd never visited the church.

The counselor talked about their services and asked questions about my daily routine. During that conversation, at about ten thirty in the morning, Jerome unexpectedly showed up at home. This was really unusual—he typically didn't get off work until five thirty in the evening—but he had to get some papers for work he'd forgotten at home. I believe God is in everything that happens, and maybe he allowed Jerome to forget those papers so he would be there right when I needed him.

"Who are you talking to?" he asked.

"Just the people at the suicide hotline center," I responded. "I was lonely and told them I was new in town. I wanted someone to talk to."

"The *suicide* hotline?" Then he noticed the drink in my hand. "It's really early to be drinking, Carolyn," Jerome said.

I said nothing in reply.

At that moment, I believe Jerome understood that a tremendous struggle was going on inside me. He may not have known what it was, but he instinctively knew it was there. And he knew I needed a doctor.

Jerome said, "Carolyn, if you don't want to talk with me about the problem, then would you please speak with your doctor? Tell him about your recurring hand rashes, your depression, and whatever you wanted to share with the suicide hotline folks."

I reluctantly agreed. But I really saw no need. I felt it would be a waste of time and money. But I made the appointment because I'd promised Jerome I would.

The doctor examined me and wasted no time telling me his diagnosis: "Well, you can keep going like you are going, and you might live another five years. Or you can accept the life that God has laid out before you and get on with living it."

Additional conversations with my doctor helped me understand that my behavior had become harmful to me. Little by little, I was self-destructing. I would have to decide that the life God had given me was worth living and that it was, in fact, his plan for me—no matter that the voices in my head tried to convince me otherwise. I believed in my heart it was true—that I could let God redeem my past. But could I live with that decision? Could I live without it?

CHAPTER 19

TURNING POINTS

⊕

I have been young, and now am old; yet have I not seen the righteous forsaken, nor his seed begging bread.

PSALM 37:25, KJV

We must seek, above all, a world of peace; a world in which people dwell together in mutual respect and work together in mutual regard.

JOHN F. KENNEDY

I THOUGHT A LOT ABOUT MY GRANDFATHER during the years we lived in Atlanta. Granddaddy had joined Mama Lessie in heaven in 1971. He suffered a stroke while alone at his home in Clanton, Alabama, managing to drag himself to the telephone, grab the cord, and pull the receiver off its cradle. In those days, an operator came on the line automatically whenever a phone came off the hook. The operator identified Granddaddy's number and called Tom Dickerson, a man who lived across the street. Tom just happened to be the neighbor Granddaddy had given his only extra front-door key, in case he ever locked himself out of the house.

Tom found my grandfather lying on the floor and got him to a small hospital in Clanton. My mother then transferred Granddaddy to Princeton Hospital, where my grandmother had died fourteen years earlier. By 1971 Princeton Hospital had integrated, so doctors allowed Granddaddy a room on the hospital's patient floor.

While in the hospital, Granddaddy's health seemed to be getting better. He looked forward to going back home. People in the churches he pastored and in his neighborhood needed him.

My grandfather joked with the nurses and talked with people all over the hospital. When I came to visit, he'd tell the nurses, "See, I told you I had a pretty granddaughter!"

But like Mama Lessie, Granddaddy never left Princeton Hospital. At the end of two weeks, he suffered another stroke and died.

I lost a good friend when my grandfather passed. I missed

him and Mama Lessie so much. With their wisdom and patience and steady belief in God, they were a source of stability in my turbulent life. I don't know where I'd be now without their strong sense of family and their constant prayers for each of us. Granddaddy, one of fourteen children, always talked about how God had taken care of his family. He was proud that not one of them had ever been arrested and that six of them had become preachers.

I often heard my grandfather quote Psalm 37:25 when he spoke of his family: "I have been young, and now am old; yet have I not seen the righteous forsaken, nor his seed begging bread." I wished I could get Granddaddy's encouragement and advice now. We had enough food on our table, but emotionally and spiritually speaking, I felt like I was desperate, begging for sustenance. I was looking for a reason to live.

⊕

I got up one morning as usual and fed and dressed Leigh, who was five, and Joya, who had just turned a year old. Granddaddy had been gone for more than two years now, and I needed him more than ever. I thought about his deep faith in God and how he had taken every opportunity to teach me life's lessons.

"Carolyn," my grandfather used to tell me, "your name means 'strong one.'" *Oh Granddaddy, I miss you, but I'm glad you can't see me now. I'm not strong anymore. You'd be so disappointed in me.*

I took a deep breath and tried to put those thoughts behind me.

"Leigh, Joya," I called to my daughters, giving each a kiss. "You can go outside and play. But stay on the deck. Don't go in the yard or near the street."

A high-traffic road ran behind our house. I had taught both children never to go near it. I sat down in a kitchen chair and poured myself a large orange juice and vodka. As I sat there in the quiet, thoughts of Cynthia Wesley filled my mind. *You'd be twenty-five years old, too, Cynthia, if you had lived. Would you be married now and have little girls of your own?* I wondered. *How I miss you, Cynthia. We could've grown up together; we'd have been best friends for a lifetime.*

It was as if Cynthia came into the room and sat down beside me.

Perhaps soon you'll be joining me, Carolyn, she said. *Remember what your doctor told you? Five years! Five years!*

I drained the glass, trying to silence the inner voice. Then I filled the glass up again with more juice and vodka.

Five years. That's not nearly enough time to raise my two daughters.

I glanced out the kitchen window and looked at my girls. They were playing together happily on the deck. My thoughts took me back to my grandfather.

I wish I could be more like you, Granddaddy. You and Mama Lessie. You gave your life to everyone around you.

I remembered my grandfather's compassionate heart for

the poor—how he reached out to them and in Christ's name met their needs—both spiritual and financial.

Granddaddy, I miss . . .

I was brought back to reality by an almost thunderous knocking on my kitchen door. It was my next-door neighbor. I had met her and her husband before, but I had never been in their house. She was older and seemed to prefer keeping to herself.

"Your daughter was almost run over by the bus!" she shouted. "The bus driver had to stop in the middle of the street to avoid hitting her! You should keep your children inside unless you come out with them!"

She turned away from the door and headed back home. Immediately I felt angry and frightened at the same time— angry that my neighbor had rushed to judgment and scolded me, but also because I knew she was right. I should have been with the girls, watching them. Instead, I was inside drinking, trying to make *myself* feel better.

Both Joya and Leigh could have been injured—or killed! I cried inside. *If anything happened to my daughters, I would really be at a point of no return!*

I made a commitment to myself that day: *Carolyn, this is it! Today everything changes. I have reached the turning point in my drinking!*

Then I prayed, *Lord, you will have to help me. I can't do this alone. I can't do anything at all if you don't help me.*

As I stood in the basement ironing, with the girls sound asleep upstairs, I continued to pray. *Lord, remind me that you love me. Help me to appreciate the good husband you sent me and to take care of my two beautiful daughters. You have given me a good life. Thank you! Now, Lord, I repent. I want to be like you.*

And then I asked my heavenly Father, *Please take away my taste for alcohol. Can you make it like I have never tasted alcohol before? Can you touch my body and heal anything harmful I have done to myself through my drinking? And can you fix me so that I don't hurt so much when I wake up each morning? Amen.*

The next two weeks turned out to be the most critical weeks of my life. I didn't know it then, however. I came to see God's power only much later, as I looked back on the difficult journey.

I knew I needed to stop drinking, but I didn't know what that would entail. I thought I would just stop. I thought I *could* just stop. I had no idea that, in those years of trying to rid myself of sadness and depression through drinking, I had created a dependency in my body and my mind. Once I stopped drinking, reality was terrifying.

The first three days were fairly uneventful. I looked after the girls, and I took care of my responsibilities at home. On days four and five I began to think about drinking a lot. By day six, I could no longer sleep at night. On days seven through eleven, I perspired a lot. And I paced relentlessly. My best time of the day was when everyone was quiet or asleep. Even better was when Jerome worked late. He still didn't realize the full extent of my problem. I couldn't stand for anyone to touch me—my whole body felt as if it were on fire, screaming.

But somehow God allowed me to get through it—alone with him. I cried. I slept. I paced. And I yelled at anyone who came too near me. By the end of day twelve, I breathed in deeply, and I exhaled. Days thirteen and fourteen were filled with prayer and resolve to never go through this again. And somehow, at that point I knew it was over. God had helped me to win, to overcome. The demon had fled. I have not looked back since.

I am ever grateful that God allowed me to live, that he took care of me when I couldn't (and didn't know how to) take care of myself. I am grateful that he touched me before I self-destructed.

CHAPTER 20

THE FIRST ARREST

✦

Their lives were taken by unknown parties on Sept. 15, 1963, when the Sixteenth Street Baptist Church was bombed. May men learn to replace bitterness and violence with love and understanding.

MEMORIAL PLAQUE FOR THE FOUR SLAIN GIRLS,
engraved on Sixteenth Street Baptist Church

He who passively accepts evil is as much involved in it as he who helps to perpetrate it. He who accepts evil without protesting against it is really cooperating with it.

MARTIN LUTHER KING JR.

WE HAD LIVED IN ATLANTA for several years when Sears decided to transfer Jerome to Warner Robins, Georgia.

Not another move! I cried, as I thought about another change. *This will mean finding another place to live, another church to join, new community clubs to keep me busy. I just don't think I can . . .*

The telephone interrupted my thoughts.

"Caroline," my father said. "I'm glad I reached you."

"What's up, Daddy?" I asked, knowing he was excited about something. Whenever he called me Caroline, it meant he was feeling good about life in general or he was in the mood to talk. *Well, at least he's not calling me girl-child!* I thought.

"Robert Chambliss is finally going to trial for Denise McNair's murder," he told me.

"No! I can't believe it, Daddy! It's been fourteen years since Denise's death."

"Bill Baxley, Alabama's attorney general, reopened the case, and Chambliss's own niece is testifying against him. He's the first of the bombers to come to trial."

"When is the trial?"

"September. Police arrested Chambliss at his home here in North Birmingham. Finally, girl-child, maybe we'll see some justice done."

I hung up the phone and said a silent prayer: *Thank you, God, that I don't live in Birmingham.* I couldn't bear hearing or reading about the bombing details and Denise's horrible death once again. I was trying so hard to put that tragedy far behind me.

When the trial began, my father kept me informed about unfolding events at the Jefferson County Courthouse.

"I heard they called Reverend Cross as a witness," he told me. "They also called Addie's sister, Sarah, to testify."

Oh, Sarah. I'm so sorry you had to hear all the gruesome details again. How could you sit in that witness chair and look in the face of the man who killed your sister?

I imagined scared little Sarah in front of the courtroom, having to look at Robert Chambliss and reliving all the horrors of September 15, 1963.

I could never do that! I thought. *Never.*

"Poor Sarah," I told my father. "She's been through so much already."

"Yes, she has, bless her heart. Caroline, I also heard that Chambliss's niece Elizabeth Cobbs came forward in court and told her story to the judge and jury."

"Is she the woman who became a Methodist minister in Alabama?"

"Yes. She worked with the FBI shortly after the church bombing," my father said. "Apparently, before the bombing Chambliss had told her, 'Just wait until after Sunday morning. They'll beg us to let them segregate!'"

"What did he mean?"

"I guess he and the other Klan members planted the church bomb to explode on that Sunday as a threat to stop us from integrating the public all-white schools in Birmingham."

"Elizabeth Cobbs overheard Chambliss say that?"

"That's what they're claiming. Cobbs also told the jury

that after the bomb went off, she heard Chambliss say, 'It wasn't meant to hurt anybody—it didn't go off when it was supposed to.'"

"Really?"

"It sounds like maybe they set the timer wrong or something. But the jury was convinced he planted the bomb that murdered Denise and the other girls."

There's no way to know for sure about the intentions behind the bomb, but I now believe it wasn't meant to take human lives. The bomb was homemade, and it would have been impossible to determine exactly when it would explode. Based on Chambliss's best guess, it should have gone off around three or four in the morning, which would have prevented our congregation from meeting for church but would not have harmed anyone. As for the phone calls, no one knows if they were simply idle bomb threats with eerie timing or if they were true warnings from someone on the inside. Either way, though, the results were the same.

Two months later, on November 18, only two days after what would have been Denise's twenty-sixth birthday, my father telephoned me again with news about the trial.

"Caroline, the judge found Robert Chambliss guilty of murdering Denise! And he was sentenced to life in prison. I also heard that after the sentencing, Chambliss told the judge, 'Judge, I swear to God I didn't bomb that church! I never bombed nothing!'"

"I wonder if the others will ever come to trial, Daddy. After all, it took fourteen years to bring Chambliss to justice."

"I don't know, Caroline."

Daddy paused. "Do you remember what everyone used to call Robert Chambliss?"

"Yes, Daddy. We called him Dynamite Bob."

"And girl-child, do you remember how I told you children, 'You aren't to go near the white house down the street, the one across the railroad tracks going toward ACIPCO?'"

"I remember, Daddy. That's where Dynamite Bob lived."

"And Caroline, did you know that Bobby Frank Cherry lived up there too?"

We had lived on 24th Avenue. If I walked north on 24th Avenue, turned left at the corner, and walked a mere six blocks, I'd be at Dynamite Bob's house.

"Thanks for letting me know about the trial, Daddy." I hung up the phone.

Now one of the church bombers has been arrested, tried, and sentenced to prison, I thought. *But two bombers still walk the streets as free men: Thomas Blanton and Bobby Frank Cherry.*

I shivered when I envisioned the hate-filled Klan on the loose, posing a real threat against the nation's homes, churches, and neighborhoods.

While in prison, Robert Chambliss penned a handwritten letter on Kilby Correctional Facility's inmate stationery to the pastor of Sixteenth Street Baptist Church. I still have a copy of his letter:

Feb. 20, 1978

Rev. Preacher, 16th Street Babtist [sic] Church, 16th Street 6th Ave. North, Birmingham, Ala.

Dear Pastor. Read this to your Congogation [sic].
I would kneel on my mothers grave [and] pray to you
I've never bomed [sic] any thing [or] killed anybody or
bin [sic] in Tommy Blanton's car in my life so help me
God. Bill Baxley sent his investagators [sic] to Detroit
to get that woman [Elizabeth Cobbs] to come down
here and sware [sic] lies on me. He flew up there in
a National Guard plane showed her my picture and
the picture of Tommy Blanton's car [and] got her to
sware [sic] I was in his car with [the] door open and
she could idinefy [sic] me over 20 feet away by Dome
Light. Paid her 100 000 dollars. The crazy woman
wasn't crazy. She was a C.I.A. Member. My wife's
niece ant [sic] nothing. The Methodist don't ordain or
licen [sic] women to preach. They coached her on what
to say and paid her when it comes to the showdown.
There will be 5 C. I. A. Members/Police or more Rev.
Baxley is just after the colored votes. I hope a [sic] pray
the colored people have got better since [sic] than to
vote for him.

Yours truly.

R. E. Chambliss. Kilby Correctional Center Facility, Rt.

5-Box 125. Montgomery, Ala. 36109

Dynamite Bob Chambliss died in prison eight years later, on October 28, 1985. In 1994, his niece Elizabeth Cobbs (who had changed her identity and name to Petric Smith) wrote a book about her uncle, the trial, and the entire ordeal. The book was entitled *Long Time Coming*.

And indeed it was.

CHAPTER 21

BACK TO BIRMINGHAM

✦

*The heart is deceitful above all things and beyond cure. Who can
understand it?*

JEREMIAH 17:9

*Ultimately, America's answer to the intolerant man is diversity,
the very diversity which our heritage of religious freedom has inspired.*

ROBERT F. KENNEDY

We had lived in Warner Robins, Georgia, for only two years when Jerome received a notice that his company planned to relocate him. When I mentioned this to the girls, who were nine and five at the time, they were not happy. We had done this before, and we knew firsthand that leaving friends and familiar surroundings behind would not be easy. It was even harder this time because the girls were getting older and they wanted some sense of permanency and continuity in their lives.

We lived in a predominately white neighborhood in Warner Robins. We had wonderful neighbors and the girls had made lots of friends, so I was hesitant about another move so soon. This move would bring us to a total of five moves in ten years. Jerome told me we had two choices: we could move to Chicago or we could go to Birmingham.

I told him, "If you move to Chicago, you will move alone."

It was meant to be funny, and we both laughed. But I was serious, too. A part of me longed for Birmingham. The city held painful memories for me, but there were also many good ones. It was still home, and I longed to go back.

Less than a month later, we packed up and prepared to move to Birmingham. I was excited. I remembered all the good times I'd had growing up in Birmingham—at home, in the community, and at church. I would find a house, get the girls comfortable and adjusted in their new schools, find a job, rejoin my church, and begin where I had left off back in 1971. My relationship with my parents was stronger now, too—they were both retired and had time to spend with the grandchildren. And on some level, I expected a brand-new Birmingham—a friendlier and more accommodating Birmingham, where my children could experience the freedom that had been lacking for me as a child. I anticipated taking my girls to all the public facilities that had been denied to me—libraries, parks, restaurants. I thought about the old segregation rules and how it was time to put my feelings of hurt and resentment to rest.

Once we moved and had settled in, I began thinking about a job. One Monday morning I took our local phone book and selected the names of ten major companies. I sent résumés and letters to each company and requested an interview. Three of the companies called me. In September 1978 I accepted a job with BellSouth, a major telecommunications company. It was fifteen years after the bombing of Sixteenth Street Baptist Church and fourteen years after the Civil Rights Act, but this Birmingham company still had an almost totally white workforce. They were under court order to hire a certain number of black employees, but in my particular office, I was the only black person. I was shocked at how slowly things had progressed in the journey to equality. I suppose I wasn't so much angry as disappointed.

I worked in the company's tax division and loved the work. My peers were not particularly friendly, but I weathered their silence, their stares, their whispering, and even the "one-some" lunches. I came to work and focused strictly on the job I had been assigned. I made my family the focus and recipients of my intense energy. Nine months after I began working for BellSouth, our son, Brandon, was born. Talk about timing! Now I had three children, a full-time job, and parents and in-laws living close by. Life seemed complete, and I was happy—utterly worn out, but happy.

Not long after we moved, we had rejoined the church I loved so much—Sixteenth Street Baptist. My family and I attended faithfully. We walked down the aisle to the front of the church together and recommitted ourselves to God and to the church, just as I had done years before as a young girl. The congregation seemed genuinely glad to have us, and I was glad to be back. Over the coming years, I taught Sunday school and helped plan the church's summer vacation Bible school. My girls went to the same Sunday school class I had gone to, and my parents were still there. The church asked me to play a major role each year when we formally remembered the September 15 bombing. In some ways, I felt I had never left Birmingham and the church at all.

But there were some significant changes at Sixteenth Street Baptist. For one thing, membership had decreased substantially in the past decade. Not many of the old members were still there—some had died, and others had moved on. The building itself was falling into disrepair. Other than the addition of an elevator, no renovations had been done since the ones immediately following the bombing. Still, it was home.

Before long, however, interracial incidents in my neighborhood interrupted my sense of peace and serenity. Jerome and

I had chosen a home in an integrated neighborhood, some distance from where I'd grown up. But I quickly discovered that "integrated" was relative. First, I learned that the community swimming pool was private. In the predominantly white community in Georgia where we had previously lived, the swimming pool had also been private—available only to the community residents. Each new family—black or white—was welcome and was given a key to the pool and a copy of the rules. But in Birmingham, "private" had a different meaning. Here no people of color had access to this community pool. Only whites could join.

For several years Jerome took a different entrance in and out of our community to avoid driving by the segregated pool. Then we decided to borrow money and put in our own swimming pool. Ironically, our backyard pool became the "community pool." That was all right with me. I knew God expected us to share his gifts with others, and we did.

Then I learned about another race-related problem in our city—the daily fights between black and white students on the city's school buses. My children weren't old enough to ride the school bus yet, but I knew that next year, if Leigh attended the public junior high school, she would be on one of those buses. I visited Jefferson County's board of education and asked why there was a problem with fighting on the buses. I also asked, "What are you going to do to correct it?"

They told me the black and white children just "couldn't seem to get along."

So they came to a decision. They would run two buses—one for black children and one for white children. I was speechless—and angry! Later I heard that the problem on the buses came about because white students had boarded school buses wearing white sheets, mimicking the Ku Klux Klan, and black students had responded by trying to remove the sheets. Fights had broken out on the buses between the junior high school students.

Fighting among students proved even worse in the community high school. Black and white students carried mace and sprayed each other with it. They also fought during lunch and at other times. The local newspapers picked up the story, and parents started to maintain a vigilant presence at the school.

I couldn't believe it. This was exactly what I had left behind in 1965! I hadn't envisioned the same situation in Birmingham now for my own children to endure. I wanted what all parents expect for their children: for them to become happy, healthy, educated, productive citizens who contribute to American life in a positive, successful way. I wanted them to have a normal childhood—I didn't want them to have to fight or march or try to justify who they were. It had been one thing to show patience during the marches in the 1960s, but I wasn't sure I could be so calm when it concerned my children.

The following year I moved my children to private schools, where they attended for the remainder of their academic years. At these schools, the officials at least appeared to be fair and attentive to all the children, regardless of their color. This was something I desperately wanted for my children.

Ever since my return to Birmingham, I'd sensed a tension between two opposing mind-sets. One contingent in Birmingham seemed to make a serious effort to "leave the 1960s" and move forward to justice and equality for all citizens. But the other segment seemed intent on staying put—maintaining the old status quo. This saddened me, and I wondered whether we'd made the right decision in moving back to Birmingham. I knew what a tremendous price had been paid by the "innocents"—my friends—in the name of freedom. For their sakes, we couldn't afford to settle for the status quo.

Still, I saw a renewed awareness of the racial unrest of the sixties as well as an interest in the Sixteenth Street Church bombing when I returned. Alabama newspaper and television reporters began to telephone me, asking for interviews. Soon I began receiving requests for interviews from other Southern states too.

For the first time Jerome became aware of how directly I had been engaged in Civil Rights activities in Birmingham. He knew what had happened in our city in the 1960s, but he hadn't known how deeply involved I'd been. With little available to me in terms of post-trauma counseling and therapy, I had traveled this painful journey hand in hand with God alone.

"All along this Christian journey," I had sung so many times, "I want Jesus to walk with me." He had. And he'd also sent Jerome.

I have always believed, almost from the moment I met Jerome, that God sent him. Unlike many of my college friends, I was not looking for a husband when I enrolled in college. But Jerome and I discovered each other, and an unbreakable bond was created. He had a quiet yet gentle and responsible way about him—the opposite of myself. Surely God determined exactly what both Jerome and I needed in a mate, as he so often does in people's lives.

We complemented each other in all the important ways and made a great team. Jerome affirmed and accepted me unconditionally, without demanding explanations. His acceptance proved essential, since my trust in people had been so badly damaged in my early years. Jerome became my greatest support.

Little did I know how much I would still need that support for the next task God had in mind for me.

CHAPTER 22

THE CALLING

⊕

The Spirit of the Sovereign LORD is on me, because the LORD has anointed me to preach good news to the poor. He has sent me to bind up the brokenhearted, to proclaim freedom for the captives and release from darkness for the prisoners.

ISAIAH 61:1

Christians should be ready for a change because Jesus was the greatest changer in history.

RALPH ABERNATHY

In the spring of 2002, I continued to think about our country's race problem. My children were now grown, and Jerome and I were still in Birmingham. Some things had improved in our city since we'd moved back, and blacks now had access to more jobs and opportunities. But although schools were technically no longer segregated, in practice they were just as segregated as they'd been in 1963. Sadly, so were churches. And perhaps most troubling of all, some people's hearts hadn't changed either.

Before he died, Dr. King had told us we had moved from the Civil Rights era to the human rights era. He said the issue at hand was bigger than race—it was about the value of human beings as children of God. I incorporated this idea into many speeches I gave as I traveled around the country. I also started work as a consultant for a project that helped lift the socioeconomic status of Southern rural black women, especially the extremely impoverished in communities such as Alabama's Black Belt, rural areas of Georgia, and the Mississippi Delta. We worked with poor people and particularly seniors, with everything from tax preparation to basic economics to HIV education.

During this time I studied all the social and economic justice information I could get my hands on. I began to understand the value of the Universal Declaration of Human Rights, adopted by the United Nations in 1948.[1] I learned that the United States was the only member of the United Nations that had not thrown its full support behind the document. I longed for more involvement—for my country, for my city, and for myself. I prayed God would use me.

I didn't get an immediate sense of a calling from God—it was something that evolved over time. But gradually, step by step, I felt the Spirit of the Lord upon me. I knew he had anointed me to preach the gospel, to bind up the broken-hearted, and to proclaim liberty to the captives. The women in the Delta knew I had risen above the tragedy of the church bombing, and they loved and admired me for that. But I knew they needed a message that would give them true hope beyond my story. They needed something bigger they could hold on to—God's message. I wanted to make sure the message I was giving them was the right one, and that's when I started feeling the pull to go to divinity school.

If, during this time, anyone had asked me if any issues from my past were still circling overhead, I would have said an emphatic no, for I had been born again and had moved on with my life. I was just trying to do God's will.

I had no idea that my life was about to change and that my world would be turned upside down and inside out. I would once again be forced to relive the horrors of September 15, 1963.

⊕

I still worked at BellSouth, where I'd been for more than twenty years. But I had grown restless and bored with my work, and I sensed that God had a new direction in mind for me. I decided it was time to leave.

On the way home from work one day, I prayed, "Lord,

I need a sign. Can you show me something?" I thought I was asking him to help me chart a course for retirement. I didn't have any grand notions about a calling.

As I turned into my community, I noticed a large billboard I had not seen before. It read, "Faith always takes the first step." Then, as though God were sitting in the car with me, I heard a voice say, "Carolyn, it is not a faith walk if I give you a calendar."

I knew I had heard from God, and I understood what he was saying to me. The next morning I drove to work, typed my retirement letter, and presented it to my director. I never looked back.

Less than a month before my retirement went into effect, the unthinkable happened. On May 2, 2002, the Circuit Court of Jefferson County served me with a witness subpoena in the *State of Alabama v. Bobby Frank Cherry* case. It was as if a long-buried corpse had made its way out of the graveyard and was suddenly sitting in my living room.

> You are hereby ordered to appear before this court as
> noted below and continue to appear from day-to-day
> hereafter until legally excused. This order is subject
> to all judicial enforcement and sanction.

The subpoena ordered me to appear in court at 9:00 a.m. on May 6, 2002—to testify on behalf of Bobby Frank Cherry! Initially, I misunderstood the subpoena.

The prosecuting attorney must have sent this, I reasoned. *He wants me to talk about the church—share its history and tell my story about the bombing.*

But when I spoke with Doug Jones, the attorney for the prosecution and a friend of mine, I discovered that Bobby Cherry's attorney had subpoenaed me to testify as a witness for the *defense*!

"What?" I cried. "They want me to testify for Cherry— one of the men who killed my friends?"

I couldn't understand why Cherry's attorney would serve me with a subpoena. *Shouldn't I be testifying for the prosecutor, Jeff Wallace? Bobby Frank Cherry is responsible for planting the bomb that killed four of my friends—why would I speak out in his defense?*

My stomach knotted. *Will this ever end? Do I have it in me to handle another assault?*

For the next few days I suffered unrelenting nausea and diarrhea. I telephoned Doug Jones and asked him if I had to go to court and testify for Cherry.

"Yes, Carolyn," he told me. "If you've been served with a legal subpoena and you don't show up, the judge can have you arrested."

Arrested? Apparently I had no choice.

I tossed and turned all that night. *I can't do it,* I cried. *I can't bear to be in the same room with Cherry or look at his face.* Worse than that (and I would not have admitted this to anyone), I was afraid. Bobby Cherry might have been behind bars, but he represented a network of evil and hatred in Birmingham. I wasn't naive enough to think Klan violence was merely a thing of the past. I was afraid for my own safety and for my family. Plus, there was the fear of the unknown— I still didn't understand why Cherry's attorney had contacted me. What would I do?

My stomach was constantly upset. I heard that another person scheduled to testify in the case had received death threats. All the old fears I had long ago put to rest, which I thought were well buried and forgotten, rose up again to haunt me.

Over the years I had developed a certain comfort level with the painful events in the past. I had found a way to make peace with them, to live with them. Now the old fears returned and threatened to strangle me, to sink me back in that horrible pit of depression I'd spent years struggling to climb out of. Almost four decades had passed, but in an instant, I was fifteen again.

CHAPTER 23

THE CHERRY TRIAL

✥

[Bobby Frank Cherry was a] trucker with an eighth grade education, no upper front teeth, a "Bobby" tattoo on his arm, seven [sic] kids, and a wife he beat and cheated on.

DIANE McWHORTER[1]

He who is devoid of the power to forgive is devoid of the power to love.

MARTIN LUTHER KING JR.

Leading up to the trial, I paced around the house for days. I developed panic attacks, and my heart raced for no explainable reason. I couldn't concentrate. Nothing brought me comfort.

I had no idea what to expect when I appeared in court.

A few days before the trial, the telephone rang. I picked up the receiver and heard the voice of Rodger Dale Bass Jr., Bobby Cherry's attorney. He was calling to make sure I would be present at the trial.

"Yes," I said. "I told you I'd be there. . . . Yes, nine o'clock on the morning of May 6."

I hung up the phone and threw up my hands in disbelief. Who would have thought that, almost forty years later, I'd still be dealing with the fallout from that September day?

Even now, I don't understand why I was called to testify on Cherry's behalf. The only thing I can think of is that this was one more way to add insult to injury.

⊕

On the morning of May 6, 2002, Jerome and I drove to the courthouse. I had been sick all night. I put my hand over my heart.

"I am not sure I can do this, Jerome!" I said. Within moments, I would be face-to-face with one of the men who had murdered my friends.

Be with me, Jesus, I prayed.

You can do it, Carolyn. I'll be with you, Jesus assured me.

Jerome parked the car. When he opened my door, reporters and photographers descended on me like locusts. They stuck microphones in my face and shouted out questions. They surrounded Jerome and me, clicking their cameras, blocking our way. It felt like a nightmare.

In the chaos, Jerome quickly took off his suit jacket and covered my head with it. Then he put his arms around me and gently led me into the court building. My heart was beating so intensely that I expected it to pop out of my chest. I prayed I could answer the attorney's questions without becoming angry and without crying. I had seen only one faded newspaper photo of Bobby Frank Cherry many years before. Even then, the sight of him had sent chills down my spine.

What will it be like to see Cherry now? I wondered. *How can I sit in the same room with him?*

I also wondered what questions I'd have to answer. What could I possibly have to say in this man's defense? *No matter what they ask me,* I told myself, *I will say as little as possible.* Doug had promised he wouldn't cross-examine me. "Carolyn, just answer the questions as simply and succinctly as you can," he had instructed me.

When we stepped inside the building, guards directed me to a holding room. "Mrs. McKinstry, you can't go into the courtroom until you are called to testify."

"Can my husband come into the holding room with me?" I asked.

"No. But Mr. McKinstry can go into the courtroom."

Jerome hugged me and reassured me and then walked into

the courtroom. Guards escorted me to a small room filled with Bobby Cherry's family members, neighbors, and friends.

Everyone looked at me—the only black person—when I entered the room. I wondered if they, too, hated black people. I wasn't angry with Cherry or his family, but I resented the situation. Out of consideration for me and what I'd been through, I felt I should have been placed in a separate room.

"If you don't know anything about Harley Davidsons," one of the men said, "then you're probably not going to fit in here very well." He then introduced himself as Bobby Cherry's pastor.

I glanced at the man out of the corner of my eye. He wore a worn leather jacket and black boots that came clear up to his knees. He had pulled his stringy, greasy hair into a long ponytail that hung down the nape of his neck.

"I am quite familiar with motorcycles. My son has a Honda 150," I told him.

Then a young man no older than twenty, dressed in a military uniform, looked my way and said a soft hello. I returned his greeting. Later I found out the young man was Cherry's grandson.

We all sat together in the small room, trying to avoid one another's eyes. No one said another word. Every now and then the bailiff walked into the dead-quiet room and called a name. "It's your turn to take the witness stand," he would say.

I tried hard to remain composed as we sat in stony silence while I waited for the bailiff to call my name.

The Lord is my shepherd, I shall not be in want.

"Mrs. Carolyn Maull McKinstry," the bailiff finally called. "It's your turn to take the witness stand."

He makes me lie down in green pastures.

I followed the bailiff into the courtroom and took the oath.

He leads me beside quiet waters, he restores my soul.

I swore to tell the truth, the whole truth.

He guides me in paths of righteousness for his name's sake.

I sat down in the witness chair beside the judge.

Even though I walk through the valley of the shadow of death . . .

Bobby Frank Cherry sat directly in front of me, only ten feet away.

I will fear no evil, for you are with me.

I felt like a knife had cut deep into the old painful wound, sliced open the healed scar, and caused it to bleed freely once again.

Your rod and your staff, they comfort me.

I looked at Bobby Frank Cherry's face.

Cherry fixed his steel-cold eyes on mine, and like a snake, his eyes never blinked, never moved. His expression—blank and hard—never changed as I answered the attorney's questions.

"Mrs. McKinstry," Mr. Bass asked. "Where were you on Sunday, September 15, 1963?"

I answered his questions as directly and honestly as I could. The questions were fairly straightforward: "What did you see that morning at church? Where were you standing when the explosion occurred?"

I looked away from Cherry's emotionless face as much as

I could. But every time I glanced back his way, Bobby Frank Cherry's eyes were locked on mine. In those eyes, I sensed all the hate and bitterness directed toward me.

You're trying to intimidate me, Mr. Cherry. And you're succeeding. I still couldn't figure out why the defense had called me to testify. Was this some sort of cruel joke?

You prepare a table before me in the presence of my enemies.

As I sat in that chair in front of the judge, the attorney, and the defendant and answered question after question, I saw in my mind's eye the faces of my four dead friends. Then I focused my eyes on the face of their murderer. As Cherry stared point-blank at me, the events of Sunday, September 15, 1963, assaulted me all over again.

The thunderous boom.

The window glass shattering and falling to the floor.

The eerie silence shrouding the church.

The command to "hit the floor!"

The church members screaming, "My children! My children!"

My two brothers, nowhere to be found.

The police cars surrounding the church.

The evening news showing stretchers covered in white sheets, carrying the burned, mutilated bodies of my four friends to the morgue.

Like a flash flood, it came rushing back, threatening to overwhelm me. I again heard my mother's words: "There were four little girls in the restroom who never made it out. They're all dead."

I yearned to leave the witness chair, to break away from Cherry's fixed glare.

I spoke only the truth as I remembered it. Not a word I said helped Cherry. Before I stepped down and ended my testimony, a new fear took hold of my heart. I was older and more experienced than I'd been in 1963. I knew how violent Klan members could be. I knew what they were capable of doing to black people—even in the twenty-first century. What would happen to me?

Cherry's eyes never stopped shouting out silent death threats. They held me in a hypnotic vice that felt as if it were about to crush me.

Even though I walk through the valley of the shadow of death, I will fear no evil, for you are with me; your rod and your staff, they comfort me.

"Thank you, Mrs. McKinstry," the judge said. "You can step down now."

Before I left, I looked again at Cherry's face. I tried hard to find some type of goodness about him. I searched deep for some sign of sympathy or sadness or remorse for the lives he had cut short, for the pain he had caused so many people. But I found nothing in that face but evil.

Jerome later told me that during the trial Cherry's ex-wife and granddaughter testified against him. They said he had boasted about the bombing.

"He said he lit the fuse," Cherry's ex-wife told the jury.

Prosecutors showed a videotape of a mob of white men beating Reverend Fred Shuttlesworth. The *Washington Post* later described the scene in the courtroom: "Prosecutors froze the film as a slender white man with a bulbous nose, wavy hair and a cigarette dangling from his mouth—unmistakably a young Bobby Frank Cherry—was seen slamming his fist into the minister's head after pulling what appeared to be a set of brass knuckles from his back pocket."[2]

A jury of nine whites and three blacks convicted Mr. Cherry of four counts of murder and sentenced him to life in prison. After the verdict, circuit judge James Garrett asked Cherry if he had anything to say.

"This whole bunch lied all the way through this thing," Cherry said. "Now, I don't know why I'm going to jail for nothing. I didn't do anything."[3]

On November 18, 2004, Bobby Frank Cherry, seventy-four, died in prison from cancer.

⊕

A few days after Cherry's trial ended, my friend Mrs. Alpha Robertson—Carole's brokenhearted mother—quietly passed away. She finally found freedom after four decades of un-bearable grief. I guess Mrs. Robertson just couldn't leave this earth until she knew Carole's killers had been caught and punished.

During Bobby Frank Cherry's trial, I had to relive those past violent and tragic days in Birmingham's history. Some might say I would have been completely justified to feel hatred, unforgiveness, and bitterness against the white people who had killed my friends and against all those who closed the doors of opportunity for generations of African-Americans.

But I discovered early in life—from my grandparents, my pastor, and others—that in God's eyes, no life should be lived in hatred or unforgiveness. Bitterness hurts only the people whose hearts house it, not the offenders.

By God's grace, I chose to forgive Bobby Frank Cherry, Robert Chambliss, Thomas Blanton, Herman Cash (a suspect who had died during the time the investigation was reopened), and all the others who lived lives of hate. It's the difficult road, yet it's also the road to ultimate freedom.

⊕

At the end of May 2002, my retirement from BellSouth became effective. I was ready—the joy of working there was now gone, and I sensed that God had something else in store for me. As I packed up my desk and said good-bye to friends, a chapter of my life closed that day. But almost immediately, a new one opened.

During the late 1970s and the 1980s, Birmingham's black mayor, Richard Arrington, had conceived the idea of building a Civil Rights museum as a place to display and store historical documents, photographs, correspondence, reports, and other memorabilia that recounted the dark and difficult Civil Rights struggle in the South, particularly in Birmingham. He shared his dream with a group of black and white Birmingham citizens, who eagerly offered their support. Their desire was to take the lessons the city had learned during the violent struggle for Civil Rights and create a place that would "encourage communication and reconciliation of human rights issues worldwide, and . . . serve as a depository for Civil Rights archives and documents." Led by Charles McCrary, the president and CEO of Alabama Power, Birmingham citizens raised $6.3 million. With support from the city, as well as Birmingham's black and white businesses, the Birmingham Civil Rights Institute* opened its doors to the public in 1992.[4]

I served on the board of directors of the Civil Rights Institute, and along with other volunteers, I frequently led tours through the Institute and the church and spoke to groups about the history of Birmingham and the struggle for Civil Rights. During that time God gave me a renewed vision for the church—both the physical building and his people. As a community, we have a charge to care for the building, because this is where we come to do the Lord's work. We have inherited this structure and the history it contains, and we need to take care of it. But at the same time, *we* are the true church, not the building. God's love resides inside *us*, so whenever we go out into the world, we take the church with us. God showed me that yes, I need to be part of the physical church, but I also need to take his love outside the church walls.

---

* Since its opening in 1992, the Civil Rights Institute has had more than 1,700,000 people from all over the world pass through its doors. It is estimated that 95 percent of them come to Birmingham specifically to tour the Institute.

✦

After the bomb exploded on September 15, 1963, shaking the church's foundation and shattering its windows, people gave funds to repair Sixteenth Street Baptist Church. But many years had passed since then, and the church was once again in desperate need of repair. The old roof leaked. The wood had rotted around the windows, allowing rain to pour inside. The sanctuary carpets remained damp most of the time. The foundation had shifted, leaving deep crevices in the walls. In a word, the church was a mess.

One day, as I led a group of tourists through the church, I noticed a healthy crop of mushrooms growing out of the once-beautiful red carpet near the pulpit. That was the final straw—I knew something had to be done.

I also knew the problem wouldn't be easily solved. Church membership had dropped drastically in recent years, and there was no money for repairs. While I pondered the problem and tried to figure out a solution, I came across a letter in the church's archives. Written by Pastor C. L. Fisher to a new member, the letter was dated August 3, 1926.

My dear Friend:

You have come into the fellowship of Sixteenth Street Baptist Church. I am very glad to have you here with us. Your presence means much to the Church, and the Church means much to you.

The church building and equipment and even the
spirit of the whole program are inherited possessions
of ours. This is our church, but it cost something. The
spirit of love cost Jesus his life. This is the spirit which
keeps the Church alive, and assures its triumph.

I paused from reading and looked at the church's cracked walls and wet carpet. *What will it cost us,* I wondered, *to repair this church and keep it going?*

Jesus paid it all, that the atmosphere of higher things
might be breathed by every living man. Buildings and
equipment cost the men and women of the past and
present no little effort. The Ministers and people of the
past are glad to hand to us this "Our Sixteenth Street."
They were mindful of us.

I thought about all the people who had sacrificed time, money, and energy to build the grand old church and to furnish it with everything they needed to worship God as a community.

We must be mindful of the present and coming
generations. To do this in the right way, we must make
a full and rounded effort to offer to God and the future,
a better Sixteenth Street.

The pastor then made a written appeal to his new member:

You are urged to help in this. The way is simple:
Consecrate your life to God. Attend the services
of your Church, especially the prayer services. Be

loyal to your God; your Church, and its program.
Be liberal in your giving, realizing that the future
generation must inherit great things, that they might
know how close we lived to God. Don't forget to pray
for your Church's success, and for the blessings of God
to be ever upon your Minister.

Yours in His Name,
C. L. Fisher

"Dear Lord!" I said when I finished reading. It was as if Pastor Fisher had written this letter specifically to me! Surely what had been true for Sixteenth Street Baptist Church in 1926 was still true in 2002!

God spoke clearly to me through the pastor's yellowed letter.

"Lord," I prayed, "through Pastor Fisher's appeal, are you showing me the more important work you want me to do for you, for your people, and for your Kingdom?"

Yes, child, he spoke to my heart.

I put the letter down. "But, Lord," I asked, "how can we repair the church and make it better for future generations if we have no money?"

You can raise the money, Carolyn, God said to my spirit.

Me? Raise the money? "It will take millions of dollars to repair this church, Lord! I have no idea how to raise that kind of money!"

God sent to me, and to our church, a huge blessing in the form of Dr. Neal Berte, a retired president of Birmingham-

Southern College. I expressed to him my vision for the church and the needs I saw, and he helped me start a campaign in Birmingham to raise the money. He encouraged me and taught me how to approach people around our city and state and ask for their help. In my view, this wasn't just a reconstruction campaign; it was part of the bigger vision for reconciliation in our city. I felt that God was calling me to be part of this effort to bring people together, to demonstrate a tangible expression of interracial progress.

It seemed that everyone I talked with wanted to donate money to the cause—individuals, corporations, and foundations. In a relatively short time, they contributed almost $4 million! In my eyes, one of the biggest blessings was that the campaign crossed all socioeconomic, religious, political, racial, gender, and age boundaries. Many donors had never had the opportunity to make a public statement for Civil Rights. They considered this fund-raising campaign an opportunity to do so.

With $4 million in the Sixteenth Street Foundation Inc. treasury, I told Jerome, "Now there will always be resources to maintain Sixteenth Street Baptist Church, to keep it alive, to keep telling the story."

The foundation hired architects and construction crews to complete the extensive renovations. In the midst of the repairs, the architect posted a sign at the church—a statement that perhaps said it all: "A restoration of hope!" Dr. Berte later told the *Birmingham News*, "We weren't sure we could get the money. I think it's a tremendous testimony to Birmingham—it speaks volumes about how far our city has come."[5]

When I stepped back and looked at the newly restored church, it truly felt like a piece of God's work of redemption. The place that had once been the site of lives lost was once again a place of new life. The place that had been a marker of hatred and despair was now a symbol of hope and reconciliation. The history and legacy of Sixteenth Street Baptist Church would be forever visible—a tall, stately sign of struggle, sacrifice, and triumph.

But our work was not finished. Now that the outer structure was once again secure, Dr. Berte and I wondered whether the church, with its rich history and its role in the Civil Rights movement, should be listed as a national historic landmark. That would qualify it to receive federal funds so it would remain strong, stable, and safe for future generations. Through the untiring efforts of Marjorie White, president of the Birmingham Historical Society, the church earned the national historic landmark status. It fell to me to fly to Washington, D.C., to address the United States Department of the Interior Committee on National Historic Landmarks. I told them the church's story and why we thought the church should be considered for this national status. I recounted the details of the church bombing, recalling that September morning somberly.

The committee listened. And they agreed. In 2006, Sixteenth Street Baptist Church became a national historic landmark. The United States attorney general, Alberto Gonzales, brought the landmark paperwork and plaque to the church himself.

❖

Every day, 365 days a year, people come from all over the world to visit Sixteenth Street Baptist Church. They want to see the place and touch the building where courageous people died in the struggle for freedom. The church remains a symbol of hope for all who enter its doors. The church does have a history marred by pain and loss, but it has also inherited a legacy of hope, love, and reconciliation.

Dr. Martin Luther King Jr. once said, "I like to believe that the negative extremes of Birmingham's past will resolve into the positive and utopian extreme of her future; that the sins of a dark yesterday will be redeemed in the achievements of a bright tomorrow."[6]

God is capable of redeeming even the ugliest and darkest moments from our past. But sometimes we first have to be willing to go back and face some of those painful places again. For example, if I'd had my way, I would never have set foot in Princeton Hospital again. But in the roundabout way in which God often works, I did find myself back there . . . some forty years after Mama Lessie's death and thirty years after Grandaddy had died there.

In the early years of the twenty-first century, I was getting my seminary degree at Birmingham's Beeson Divinity School on the campus of Samford University—something I wouldn't have been able to do just a generation ago. During the course of my master of divinity classes, I journeyed back to Princeton Hospital for an internship. It was something my soul insisted I do. I had "unfinished business" there, and I needed to deal with it head-on. This time, however, I visited not as the little girl in the corner of the basement when Mama Lessie had died but as a hospital chaplain.

The hospital had long been desegregated by this point. In my rounds as a part-time chaplain, I often thought back to those sad, frightening days when Mama Lessie lay dying in the unfinished basement. Now, as one of God's servants, I could provide spiritual and tangible comfort to those who needed it, without regard to color or religion. I could offer love and support during their times of illness and bereavement because I knew what it was like to be there. In his divine knack for bringing things full circle, God called me to do for others what had not been done for my grandmother.

The deaths of my four girlfriends left me with a pain I cannot describe. But something beautiful has come of it, and that's the vision God has given for reconciliation. My passion is to see people learn to work together and appreciate the diversity God created among us. This has become a calling for me, and I think about it all the time. I have been given opportunities to answer this call in my own city in smaller, daily ways. But I also receive national and international invitations to share that same passion for reconciliation in our world.

In the 1960s, it seemed as though reconciliation was primarily about blacks and whites. But today it's even broader, and it really comes down to interactions between individuals. The core of the issue is still the same, however. I believe that if we can't learn to live with our brothers and sisters here on earth, how will we get a chance to work it out in heaven? I also believe that one good deed begets another good deed and that if we all adopt a spirit of love toward our neighbors and toward each individual we encounter, we can slowly make this world a better place—a place of reconciliation, as God intended.

It has been more than forty years since my friends were killed, and we've made some progress in that time. But I have a greater vision for the next forty years—a vision of building a society where the lamb can truly lie with the lion and there will be peace.

I'm reminded of one of the classic hymns we used to sing at Sixteenth Street Baptist Church: "It Is Well with My Soul."

When peace, like a river, attendeth my way,
When sorrows like sea billows roll;
Whatever my lot, Thou has taught me to say,
It is well, it is well, with my soul. . . .

And Lord, haste the day when my faith shall be sight,
The clouds be rolled back as a scroll;
The trump shall resound, and the Lord shall descend,
Even so, it is well with my soul.

At this point in my life, I am able to imagine Addie, Cynthia, Denise, and Carole perched on a cloud somewhere in the sky, their arms around each other, looking down at the church. And it is clear to them that all is well. They are waving their hands and saying, "Carry on! Carry on! It is well with our souls."

And it is also well with my own soul.

EPILOGUE

For many years I hated those Klan members who bombed my church and killed my four young friends. I wondered how they could do what they did—hurt innocent people because of their skin color. I was angry and confused, and I felt powerless to fix the problem. Hatred, unforgiveness, and bitterness were eating me up, slowly destroying me.

When I was a child and a young adult, it hadn't really occurred to me that I needed to forgive Klan members. I learned, however, that the hate I held in my heart was hurting me, not them. I cried regularly for twenty years after the bombing. Every time I saw something that reminded me of my friends' deaths, I relived all the past pain and sorrow. In my anger and hurt, I became dependent on alcohol to numb my inner pain, and I couldn't sleep at night. I spent years struggling with depression and strained relationships before I was finally able to release this hatred that I harbored in my heart.

I'll never forget the day I fell on my knees and prayed a specific prayer of surrender: "God, I don't know what I've done to myself—the smoking, the drinking, the sleepless nights. I have become a nervous wreck. Please, God, give me the strength to put it all down. Please fix my body and take away my cravings for alcohol. Please touch me with your healing so I can go forward, knowing I've left behind all the unforgiveness in my heart." That prayer was the beginning of the healing process for me. I made a conscious choice that day to forgive the men who had caused me, my family, my friends, and my community such fear and pain.

I still had much to learn about forgiveness, however—that was only the first step. I didn't know how it worked, why it healed, what Scripture said about it. I had a lot of growing and maturing to do, and they didn't happen overnight. Even now, when my memory returns to those dark, frightening times, I must go back to God in prayer and ask him to keep unforgiveness from my heart and to help me see offending people through his eyes, not my own. I know that because of the way Christ has forgiven me, I have no option but to forgive others who have intentionally hurt me and those I love.

At its core, forgiveness is a spiritual act—it's not something we can do in our own strength. As a Christian woman who has been forgiven by God, I have come to understand that God created all of us—including Bobby Frank Cherry, Thomas Blanton, Robert Chambliss, and Governor George Wallace—even though their hearts overflowed with hate and they allowed that hate to dictate their cruel actions. I have also learned that just as God loves me, he also loves all the people he created. He does not love the crimes they commit, the disrespectful language they use, the bitterness they nurture in their hearts, or the pain and suffering they bring to others. But he loves *them*.

I have often read and reflected on the Bible's account of Jesus' crucifixion (see Luke 23:33-43). From the cross, Jesus looked down on the men who crucified him and prayed, "Father, forgive them, for they do not know what they are doing" (Luke 23:34). On each side of Jesus, two common criminals—both deserving of their punishment—had also been nailed to wooden crosses. One thief insulted Jesus. The other criminal, however, rebuked the insulting thief, saying, "This man has done nothing wrong" (Luke 23:41). Then the criminal looked toward the dying Jesus and made a request of deep faith: "Jesus, remember me when you come into your kingdom." Jesus answered him, "I tell you the truth, today you will be with me in paradise" (Luke 23:42-43).

Jesus forgave the men who crucified him as well as the thief who hung beside him. Pondering that Scripture, as well as other passages throughout the Bible, I came to understand that I, too, needed to forgive those who had hurt me and my family and friends. And that forgiveness was more important for me than for them. It allowed me to move forward with the life God had planned for me. During those times of prayer, Scripture reading, and reflection God seemed to touch my heart. He helped me through the long process of forgiveness, and by his grace I chose to sincerely forgive all those who had so profoundly impacted my young life. Once I forgave, the burden I had carried in my heart lifted. I began to see people the way God sees them. When I stepped into the witness box in that courtroom some forty years after Bobby Cherry had bombed my church, I looked at the man in a different way. Though I was still afraid of him, I could also see another side to him. He looked like an old, tired—albeit hate-filled—grandfather, not the murderer of four innocent Sunday school girls.

I know all of us are capable of evil, but I also believe that as people made in God's image, there is also good in all of us. Surely we must become intentional in looking for that good.

Loving Our Neighbors

One of the biggest lessons in forgiveness I've learned is that God has called me—and each one of us—to care for our neighbors. I try to live by this Scripture verse: "Love does no harm to its neighbor" (Romans 13:10). Jesus himself had a lot to say about the way we treat our neighbors. In addition to the great commission, he also gave us one of the greatest commandments: "Love your neighbor as yourself" (Matthew 22:39). Who are our neighbors? Every person on earth, regardless of color, age, gender, or financial circumstances. What does it mean to love our neighbors? It means forgiving them when they hurt or offend us or someone we love. It means letting go of our anger and resentment against them. It means looking at them with God's eyes and seeing the goodness in them as creatures made by the almighty

Creator God. It means doing our neighbors no harm and treating them as we ourselves want to be treated.

Above all, genuine love does something—it never sits back and watches. Compassion doesn't require a large committee or a formal, organized approach. You and I can each become a "committee of one." Hurting people surround us. On each day that God gives us life, we can intentionally strive to help those who are in need. Just imagine what could happen if each one of us reached out every day and touched one person with Christ's love. One by one, healing would take place in people's hearts. I believe we can help heal the world with something as simple as daily acts of kindness.

Only about six months after the bomb blast killed my four friends at Sixteenth Street Baptist Church, in the spring of 1964, a young woman in New York City was stabbed and killed in public. Thirty-eight of her neighbors watched her murder but did nothing to help save her life. They opened their windows, looked out at the screaming woman fighting for her life, and simply watched. The woman was twenty-eight-year-old Catherine Genovese. Her neighbors called her "Kitty." She was returning home late from work one evening and a man grabbed her. Kitty cried out to the watching neighbors for help, but no one responded. The man stabbed her, and she again screamed for help: "He stabbed me! Please help me! Please help me!" The assailant ran away, and Kitty struggled to her feet. When nobody came to her aid, she continued to scream for help: "I'm dying! I'm dying!" But still no one responded. Seeing no opposition, the assailant returned and stabbed Kitty to death—while the world watched. Later, when detectives asked spectators why they didn't simply dial "0" on their phones and call the police, one person said, "I don't know." Another said, "I didn't want to get involved."[1] If we truly love our neighbors, we will protect them from others who hurt or humiliate them. We will step into their situations and take a stand for them as individuals created by God.

In order to truly love our neighbors, we have to get to know them. As we live and work and commute in the course of our busy everyday lives, we often miss opportunities to truly connect with the people who live around us. We can become so comfortable and protected in our own comfort zones that we fail to reach out to neighbors who are different from us. Genuine love sees beyond the external differences and finds the similarities of another's heart.

I once heard a beautiful illustration of loving one's neighbor. A woman in a large neighborhood was sick, had surgery, and came home to recover. Someone placed a huge ice chest on her front steps and filled it with fresh ice every morning. Each day, different people from all over the neighborhood came by and placed casseroles, cakes, soups, and other prepared food in the ice chest for the woman and her family to eat that night. These were anonymous acts of kindness that helped the woman toward physical healing and allowed her to take care of her family. True love gives without needing applause or credit.

The Birmingham Pledge

The city of Birmingham has made its mistakes over the years. People have suffered here because of human cruelties and violence toward one another. As I have pondered the struggle for Civil Rights, I have often asked myself the question *Can anything good come out of Birmingham?* I confess that at times I've doubted that anything good could ever come out of my city.

But still I cling to hope. And I know there *is* something good that has come from the pain and suffering of Birmingham's segregated, violent, dark days: the Birmingham Pledge.

Inspired by the historic events that took place in this city during the Civil Rights movement, Birmingham attorney James E. Rotch composed a statement—a personal commitment to recognize the importance of every individual, regardless of race or color. This commitment became a grassroots movement committed to eliminating prejudice in Birmingham and throughout the world. In the last five years, the Birmingham Pledge has received worldwide recognition, with signatures from tens of thousands of people. In January 2000, a joint resolution of Congress was passed recognizing the Birmingham Pledge. In 2001, President George W. Bush proclaimed September 14–21 as National Birmingham Pledge Week, and he encouraged all citizens to join him in renewing their commitment to fight racism and uphold equal justice and opportunity.

The Birmingham Pledge simply says,

- I believe that every person has worth as an individual.
- I believe that every person is entitled to dignity and respect, regardless of race or color.
- I believe that every thought and every act of racial prejudice is harmful; if it is my thought or act, then it is harmful to me as well as to others.
- Therefore, from this day forward I will strive daily to eliminate racial prejudice from my thoughts and actions.
- I will discourage racial prejudice by others at every opportunity.
- I will treat all people with dignity and respect; and I will strive daily to honor this pledge, knowing that the world will be a better place because of my effort.[2]

In signing this document, people are pledging to believe in the worth of every person God created and to treat people with respect and dignity. It is also an acknowledgment that racial discrimination—every thought and every cruel action—is harmful, both to the offender and to the recipient. So basic, so simple, and yet so life honoring.

The Gift of Forgiveness

Not long ago I was asked to speak at the Underground Railroad, a historic Civil Rights museum in Cincinnati, Ohio.

During my visit I met the senior historian and adviser at the museum, a man in his seventies named Carl Westmoreland. He welcomed me, proudly gave me a personal tour, and showed me the museum's artifacts. Carl and I had met many years earlier, and he had heard my story of choosing to forgive the men who had killed my four friends.

"After hearing your story, Carolyn," he said, "I, too, decided to forgive the white men who had set my house on fire. I had been angry for many years, and I'd allowed my heart to fill up with hatred and bitterness. But after listening to you, there was no way I could continue to hold on to that bitterness. I knew I had to forgive."

Then Carl told me his story. He had owned a house in an impoverished and fairly rough part of downtown Cincinnati. Developers eyed the property and decided they wanted to buy it so they could turn it into apartment buildings. Carl, however, turned down their offer. After many attempts on the developers' part and Carl's continual refusal to sell, someone went to Carl's home while he was at work and set his house on fire. Carl's eight-year-old son was home alone at the time. The boy managed to get out alive and unharmed, but Carl knew his son could have been burned to death. Over the years Carl hadn't let go of his anger at this cruel act, and instead had allowed hatred, resentment, and bitterness to grow unchecked in his heart.

That day, during my visit to the Underground Railroad, Carl confessed to me, "When I heard you speak, I realized that if you could forgive those men who had bombed your

FROM MARTIN LUTHER KING JR.'S "WHERE DO WE GO FROM HERE?" SPEECH

I'm concerned about a better world. I'm concerned about justice; I'm concerned about brotherhood; I'm concerned about truth. And when one is concerned about that, he can never advocate violence. For through violence you may murder a murderer, but you can't murder murder. Through violence you may murder a liar, but you can't establish truth. Through violence you may murder a hater, but you can't murder hate through violence. Darkness cannot put out darkness; only light can do that.

And I say to you, I have also decided to stick with love, for I know that love is ultimately the only answer to mankind's problems. And I'm going to talk about it everywhere I go. I know it isn't popular to talk about it in some circles today. And I'm not talking about emotional bosh when I talk about love; I'm talking about a strong, demanding love. For I have seen too much hate. I've seen too much hate on the faces of sheriffs in the South. I've seen hate on the faces of too many Klansmen and too many White Citizens Councilors in the South to want to hate, myself, because every time I see it, I know that it does something to their faces and their personalities, and I say to myself that hate is too great a burden to bear. I have decided to love. If you are seeking the highest good, I think you can find it through love. And the beautiful thing is that we aren't moving wrong when we do it, because John was right, God is love. He who hates does not know God, but he who loves has the key that unlocks the door to the meaning of ultimate reality.

And so I say to you today, my friends, that you may be able

to speak with the tongues of men and angels; you may have the eloquence of articulate speech; but if you have not love, it means nothing. Yes, you may have the gift of prophecy; you may have the gift of scientific prediction and understand the behavior of molecules; you may break into the storehouse of nature and bring forth many new insights; yes, you may ascend to the heights of academic achievement so that you have all knowledge; and you may boast of your great institutions of learning and the boundless extent of your degrees; but if you have not love, all of these mean absolutely nothing. You may even give your goods to feed the poor; you may bestow great gifts to charity; and you may tower high in philanthropy; but if you have not love, your charity means nothing.

And if you will let me be a preacher just a little bit. One day, one night, a juror came to Jesus and he wanted to know what he could do to be saved. Jesus didn't get bogged down on the kind of isolated approach of what you shouldn't do. Jesus didn't say, "Now Nicodemus, you must stop lying." He didn't say, "Nicodemus, now you must not commit adultery." He didn't say, "Now Nicodemus, you must stop cheating if you are doing that." He didn't say, "Nicodemus, you must stop drinking liquor if you are doing that excessively." He said something altogether different, because Jesus realized something basic: that if a man will lie, he will steal. And if a man will steal, he will kill. So instead of just getting bogged down on one thing, Jesus looked at him and said, "Nicodemus, you must be born again." . . .

What I'm saying today is that we must go from this convention and say, "America, you must be born again!"[3]

283

church, murdered your friends, and almost killed you, I knew I had no choice but to forgive the men who had burned down my house and could have killed my son."

He told me, "Carolyn, when I looked at you as you spoke, I saw a light in you. You reflected such joy and peace. At that time, I was miserable. I hadn't been able to get past the pain and the anger. I still thought everyone was out to hurt me."

Forgiveness had been a long process for Carl, too, but he had chosen to take that path. He went on to live a life worthy of God and filled with new purpose. What a marvelous and mighty God who raised Carl to his position at the Underground Railroad. He became one of the "wounded healers."

✦

As I raised my three children, I tried to teach them to give the gift of forgiveness to those who hurt them. I told them my story—the details of the church bombing and the murder of my friends. I checked out library books and read them the historical accounts of the bombing, the Civil Rights marches, and Dr. King's work. I wanted them to be conscious that we live in a fallen world and that everything is not well on planet Earth. I tried to prepare them for possible racial injustices and hate-filled people. I wanted them to understand what it means to make the choice to forgive others who might hurt them.

Sometimes people ask me if the price of forgiveness is worth it. But God has rewarded me beyond my expectations for choosing to forgive. He has filled my heart with an overflowing love for people—black, white, whatever their color or culture. God took away the bitterness that, like an unattended garden weed, might have grown in my heart over the years and choked out joy and purpose in my life. He has given me a ministry of love and reconciliation that wouldn't have been possible if bitterness had remained rooted in me. God has used my story of pain and suffering as a witness to how love can overcome hate, how forgiveness can overcome bitterness, and how joy can overcome pain.

It's Time to Stop Watching

As I ponder on the title of this book, *While the World Watched,* I see that the world has stood back passively and watched people hurt other people for many years. But now I believe it is time for us to stop watching. It is time for us, with God's help, to take action. For some reason, God has chosen to use imperfect individuals like us to bring about his will and his Kingdom purposes on this fragile planet. I am convinced that through the intentional actions of caring, concerned individuals we will see healing take place in this world.

Our society has taken down the signs on the public toilets and water fountains, but the battle is not yet won. Governments and organizations haven't been able to erase human suffering on earth. I have come to understand that hearts must be changed one person at a time in order to truly put racial prejudices and violence behind us. The better way—the only way—is the personal way. The only hope for true transformation is for concerned, compassionate individuals to stop watching and decide to become ambassadors of forgiveness, peace, and reconciliation. Only God can change hearts, but he can use us and our stories to reach out and touch those in need of healing.

As believers in Jesus Christ, our responsibility is to teach God's love and forgiveness to a world where injustice and pain often rule. We must show the way of love—love for God and love for our neighbors. We as a people can no longer be silent. We must speak out in love and speak out against those things that hurt others.

For many years we have seen the effects of hate on our world. Now it is time to prove what love will do. One day at a time, one individual at a time, and one act of kindness at a time—we can heal the world. We must stop watching and begin healing.

Sample Jim Crow Laws

- Colored persons may not address white persons by their given names; they must always use titles of respect (e.g., Mr., Mrs., Miss, Sir, or Ma'am). Whites must not use courtesy titles of respect when referring to blacks. Instead, blacks must be called by their first names.
- Blacks must be introduced to whites, never whites to blacks. For example, "Mr. Peters [the white person], this is Charlie [the black person], about whom I spoke to you."
- A black man cannot offer his hand to shake with a white man because it implies social equality. A black male is forbidden from offering his hand or any other part of his body to a white woman.[1]
- It shall be unlawful to conduct a restaurant or other place for the serving of food in the city at which white and colored people are served in the same room, unless such white and colored persons are effectually separated by a solid partition extending from the floor upward to

a distance of seven feet or higher, and unless a separate
entrance from the street is provided.

- All persons licensed to conduct a restaurant shall
  serve either white people exclusively or colored people
  exclusively and shall not sell to the two races within the
  same room or under the same license.[2]
- Colored people must sit in the backseat or in the back of
  a truck driven by a white person.
- When crossing an intersection, a black driver must always
  give the right-of-way to the white driver.[3]
- Negroes are to be served through a separate branch
  or branches of the county free library, which shall be
  administered by a custodian of the Negro race under the
  supervision of the county librarian.
- The state librarian is directed to fit up and maintain a
  separate place for the use of the colored people who may
  come to the library for the purpose of reading books or
  periodicals.[4]
- No person or corporation shall require any white female
  nurse to nurse in wards or rooms in hospitals, either
  public or private, in which negro men are placed.
- The board of trustees shall maintain a separate building,
  on separate grounds, for the admission, care, instruction,
  and support of all blind persons of the colored or black
  race.
- There shall be maintained by the governing authorities
  of every hospital maintained by the state for treatment of
  white and colored patients separate entrances for white

and colored patients and visitors, and such entrances shall be used by the race only for which they are prepared.[5]

- All passenger stations in this state operated by any motor transportation company shall have separate waiting rooms or space and separate ticket windows for the white and colored races.

- The conductor of each passenger train is authorized and required to assign each passenger to the car or the division of the car, when it is divided by a partition, designated for the race to which such passenger belongs.

- All railroad companies are hereby required to provide separate cars or coaches for the travel and transportation of the white and colored passengers.[6]

- All circuses, shows, and tent exhibitions, to which the attendance of more than one race is invited shall provide not less than two ticket offices and not less than two entrances.

- Any public hall, theatre, opera house, motion picture show, or place of public entertainment which is attended by both white and colored persons shall separate the white race and the colored race.[7]

- Separate schools must be established for the education of children of African descent. It is unlawful for colored children to attend any white school or any white children to attend a colored school.

- School textbooks must not be exchanged between the white and colored schools.[8]

- If an instructor teaches in any school, college, or

institution where white and colored students are enrolled as pupils, he will be deemed guilty of a misdemeanor, and upon conviction, be fined.[9]

- It shall be unlawful for a Negro and white person to play together or in company with each other at any game of pool or billiards.
- It shall be unlawful for any amateur white baseball team to play on any vacant lot or baseball diamond within two blocks of a playground devoted to the Negro race, and it shall be unlawful for any amateur colored baseball team to play baseball within two blocks of any playground devoted to the white race.[10]

Letter from Barack Obama

to the Sixteenth Street Baptist Church, Birmingham

SEPTEMBER 15, 2008

Dear Friends,

Thank you for the opportunity to share a few thoughts as we gather here today to remember four little girls tragically taken from us in 1963, and to congratulate you on the restoration of one of the landmarks of the Civil Rights Movement in America.

I imagine that in quiet moments, many of you have thought about who Addie Mae Collins, Denise McNair, Carole Robertson, and Cynthia Wesley might have become had they been allowed to grow up. Maybe a doctor and a history teacher, a singer and a social worker— their world would have been one of increasing possibility, symbolized in no small part by this magnificent Church and the community that built and sustains it.

Much has changed in four-and-a-half decades, and our nation has made great progress. But as we gather here today, we know that so much remains to be done. We know that the Lord calls on us to keep the memory of these girls alive by fighting for justice so that we may look at each other and at ourselves and say that they have not died in vain.

On this day 45 years ago, four young souls were lost in the struggle of that time to extend our nation's promise to all of our citizens. The men who inflicted the pain on that day sought to set off a chain reaction of similar events around the South. But what man meant for evil, God used for good, and the shock and horror of that day galvanized a nation. It led to an outpouring of protest from people of all colors, and to the Civil Rights Act of 1964.

We clearly understand what the sacrifice of those young women meant for African Americans. However, we can also see how their passing allowed many whites to be led less by the laws of Jim Crow and the societal pressures that went with them, and more by their hearts in their treatment of African Americans. The Civil Rights Movement did not simply free African Americans, it freed all Americans.

The attack on this church made people stand up from the streets of Birmingham to the halls of Congress. Today, we must continue to stand against injustice and inequality. One of the best ways to honor this tragic day is to participate in the electoral process by registering new voters, recruiting new volunteers, and encouraging people to turn out on Election Day. And when we do this, we will continue the work of creating equality of opportunity for all Americans and creating a more perfect union.

That's what we can do to honor the memory of those four little girls, and to create the change we seek. On behalf of Michelle and our two little girls, God bless you all, and God bless this nation.

Sincerely,

Barack Obama

Notes

CHAPTER 1—TOO GREAT A BURDEN TO BEAR

1. Martin Luther King Jr., "Where Do We Go from Here?" August 16, 1967, Atlanta, Georgia, http://mlk-kpp01.stanford.edu/index.php/encyclopedia/documentsentry/where_do_we_go_from_here_delivered_at_the_11th_annual_sclc_convention.

CHAPTER 2—HALFWAY IN AND HALFWAY OUT

1. Martin Luther King Jr., "I Have a Dream," August 28, 1963, speech delivered on the steps at the Lincoln Memorial in Washington, D.C., http://avalon.law.yale.edu/20th_century/mlk01.asp.
2. Ibid.
3. The National Center for Public Policy Research, *Brown v. Board of Education*, 347 U.S. 483 (1954), http://www.nationalcenter.org/brown.html.
4. Connor made this statement to the Southern Conference for Human Welfare in 1938. Quoted from Diane McWhorter, *Carry Me Home* (New York: Touchstone, 2001), 158.

CHAPTER 3—THE STRONG ONE

1. Martin Luther King Jr., "I Have a Dream," August 28, 1963, delivered on the steps at the Lincoln Memorial in Washington, D.C., http://avalon.law.yale.edu/20th_century/mlk01.asp.

CHAPTER 4—THE BOMB HEARD 'ROUND THE WORLD

1. Martin Luther King Jr., "Where Do We Go from Here?" August 16, 1967, Atlanta, Georgia, http://mlk-kpp01.stanford.edu/index.php/encyclopedia/documentsentry/where_do_we_go_from_here_delivered_at_the_11th_annual_sclc_convention.

CHAPTER 5—LIFE IS BUT A VAPOR
1. United Press International, "Six Dead After Church Bombing," *Washington Post*, September 16, 1963, http://www.washingtonpost.com/wp-srv/national/longterm/churches/photo3.htm.
2. Ibid.
3. Ibid.
4. Roy Reed, "Charles Morgan Jr., 78, Dies: Leading Civil Rights Lawyer," *New York Times*, January 9, 2009, http://www.nytimes.com/2009/01/10/us/10morgan.html?_r=1.

CHAPTER 6—FOUR LITTLE COFFINS
1. Dr. Martin Luther King's funeral eulogy, Sixth Avenue Baptist Church, September 18, 1963, http://mlk-kpp01.stanford.edu/index.php/encyclopedia/documentsentry/doc_eulogy_for_the_martyred_children.
2. Ibid.
3. Ibid.

CHAPTER 7—THE AFTERMATH
1. George McMillan, "The Birmingham Church Bomber," *Saturday Evening Post*, June 6, 1964, 14–17.
2. Dr. Martin Luther King's funeral eulogy, Sixth Avenue Baptist Church, September 18, 1963, http://mlk-kpp01.stanford.edu/index.php/encyclopedia/documentsentry/doc_eulogy_for_the_martyred_children.
3. Ibid.
4. George McMillan, "The Birmingham Church Bomber," *Saturday Evening Post*, June 6, 1964, 14–17.
5. "The '63 Baptist Church Bombing," Federal Bureau of Investigation, September 26, 2007, http://www.fbi.gov/page2/sept07/bapbomb092607.htm.
6. Ibid.
7. Quote taken from a photocopy of the original letter by Reverend C. Herbert Oliver, September 20, 1963.

CHAPTER 8—THE WORLD WAS SILENT
1. Martin Luther King Jr., "Letter from Birmingham Jail," April 16, 1963, http://abacus.bates.edu/admin/offices/dos/mlk/letter.html.
2. "Timeline: The Murder of Emmett Till," *American Experience*, PBS, http://www.pbs.org/wgbh/amex/till/timeline/timeline2.html.
3. Ibid.

4. William Bradford Huie, "The Shocking Story of Approved Killing in Mississippi," *Look*, January 24,1956, http://www.pbs.org/wgbh/amex/till/sfeature/sf_look_confession.html.
5. Ibid.
6. "Killers' Confession: Letters to the Editor," *Look*, http://www.pbs.org/wgbh/amex/till/sfeature/sf_look_letters.html.
7. Harrison E. Salisbury, "Fear and Hatred Grip Birmingham," *New York Times*, April 12, 1960, http://reportingcivilrights.loa.org/authors/selections.jsp?authorId=70.
8. Harrison E. Salisbury, quoted in Terry Gross, "Get On the Bus: The Freedom Riders of 1961," NPR, January 12, 2006, http://www.npr.org/templates/story/story.php?storyId=5149667.
9. Martin Luther King Jr., "Letter from Birmingham Jail," April 16, 1963, http://mlk-kpp01.stanford.edu/index.php/resources/article/annotated_letter_from_birmingham/#outsiders.
10. Eric Pace, "Harrison E. Salisbury, 84, Author and Reporter, Dies," *New York Times*, July 7, 1993, http://www.nytimes.com/1993/07/07/obituaries/harrison-e-salisbury-84-author-and-reporter-dies.html?pagewanted=1.
11. Interview with attorney Colonel William S. Pritchard from *Who Speaks for Birmingham*, "CBS Reports," May 18, 1961.
12. Diane McWhorter, *Carry Me Home* (New York: Touchstone, 2001), 21.

CHAPTER 9—"IT'S TIME!"

1. Martin Luther King Jr., "Letter from Birmingham Jail," April 16, 1963, http://abacus.bates.edu/admin/offices/dos/mlk/letter.html.
2. "The 1963 Inaugural Address of Governor George C. Wallace," January 14, 1963, Alabama Department of Archives and History, http://www.archives.alabama.gov/govs_list/inauguralspeech.html.
3. Ibid.
4. Martin Luther King Jr., "Letter from Birmingham Jail," April 16, 1963, http://mlk-kpp01.stanford.edu/index.php/resources/article/annotated_letter_from_birmingham/#outsiders.
5. See Romans 12:1.
6. Robert Shelton, "Songs a Weapon in Rights Battle: Vital New Ballads Buoy Negro Spirits across the South," *New York Times*, August 15, 1962.

CHAPTER 10—D-DAY

1. Lisa Cozzens, "Birmingham," *African American History*, http://www.watson.org/~lisa/blackhistory/civilrights-55-65/birming.html.

CHAPTER 11—DOUBLE D-DAY

1. "Project 'C' in Birmingham," *American Experience: The Presidents,* PBS, http://www.pbs.org/wgbh/amex/eyesontheprize/story/07_c.html.

CHAPTER 12—THE MOST DANGEROUS RACIST IN AMERICA

1. "Statement and Proclamation of Governor George C. Wallace," June 11, 1963, Alabama Department of Archives and History, http://www.archives .alabama.gov/govs_list/schooldoor.html.
2. Douglas Martin, "Vivian Malone Jones, 63, Dies; First Black Graduate of University of Alabama," *New York Times,* October 14, 2005, http://www.nytimes.com/2005/10/14/national/14jones.html?_r=1.
3. Ibid.
4. John F. Kennedy, "Speech on Civil Rights," American Rhetoric, http://www.americanrhetoric.com/speeches/jfkcivilrights.htm.
5. John F. Kennedy, "Radio and Television Report to the American People on Civil Rights," June 11, 1963, http://www.jfklibrary .org/Historical+Resources/Archives/Reference+Desk/Speeches/ JFK/003POF03CivilRights06111963.htm.
6. George Wallace, "Executive Order Number Ten of the Governor of Alabama," September 9, 1963.
7. "Report on Desegregation in the Schools of Alabama," *American Experience: The Presidents,* http://www.pbs.org/wgbh/amex/presidents/35_kennedy/ psources/ps_deseg.html.
8. John F. Kennedy, "Report on Desegregation in the Schools of Alabama," September 9, 1963, http://www.pbs.org/wgbh/amex/ presidents/35_kennedy/psources/ps_deseg.html.
9. *New York Times,* September 6, 1963.

CHAPTER 13—THE BATTLE CONTINUES

1. Martin Luther King Jr., "Where Do We Go from Here?" August 16, 1967, Atlanta, Georgia, http://mlk-kpp01.stanford.edu/index.php/encyclopedia/ documentsentry/where_do_we_go_from_here_delivered_at_the_11th_ annual_sclc_convention.

CHAPTER 14—SERVANT, HEAL THYSELF

1. "Rev. Fred L. Shuttlesworth," Guide to the Twentieth Century African American Resources at the Cincinnati Historical Society Library, http://library.cincymuseum.org/aag/bio/shuttlesworth.html.
2. Dr. Martin Luther King's funeral eulogy, Sixth Avenue Baptist Church, September 18, 1963, http://mlk-kpp01.stanford.edu/index.php/ encyclopedia/documentsentry/doc_eulogy_for_the_martyred_children.

3. George McMillan, "The Birmingham Church Bomber," *Saturday Evening Post*, June 6, 1964, 14–17.

4. Martin Luther King Jr., "Where Do We Go from Here?" August 16, 1967, Atlanta, Georgia, http://mlk-kpp01.stanford.edu/index.php/encyclopedia/documentsentry/where_do_we_go_from_here_delivered_at_the_11th_annual_sclc_convention.

5. James W. Douglass, *JFK and the Unspeakable* (Maryknoll, NY: Orbis Books, 2008), 369.

6. Ibid., 368.

7. Martin Luther King Jr., "What Killed JFK?" *New York Amsterdam News*, December 21, 1963, http://mlk-kpp01.stanford.edu/index.php/encyclopedia/encyclopedia/enc_new_york_amsterdam_news.

CHAPTER 15—BOMBINGHAM

1. "Sixteenth Street Baptist Church," We Shall Overcome: Historic Places of the Civil Rights Movement, http://www.nps.gov/history/nr/travel/civilrights/al11.htm.

CHAPTER 16—WILL THE VIOLENCE EVER END?

1. "John F. Kennedy: The American Promise to African Americans," Encyclopaedia Britannica Profiles: The American Presidency, http://www.britannica.com/presidents/article-9116924.

2. Ben Chaney, "Schwerner, Chaney, and Goodman: The Struggle for Justice," American Bar Association, http://www.abanet.org/irr/hr/springoohumanrights/chaney.html.

3. "Major Features of the Civil Rights Act of 1964," The Dirksen Congressional Center, http://www.congresslink.org/print_basics_histmats_civilrights64text.htm.

4. "Richard B. Russell Jr.," The New Georgia Encyclopedia, http://www.georgiaencyclopedia.org/nge/Article.jsp?id=h-1391.

5. William Brink and Louis Harris, "The Negro Revolution in America," *Newsweek*, September 30, 1963, 26.

6. Juan Williams, *Eyes on the Prize: America's Civil Rights Years, 1954–1965* (New York: Penguin Books, 1987), 179.

7. Martin Luther King Jr., "Nobel Lecture: The Quest for Peace and Justice," http://nobelprize.org/nobel_prizes/peace/laureates/1964/king-lecture.html.

8. Martin Luther King Jr., "The Nobel Prize in Peace 1964: Acceptance Speech," http://nobelprize.org/nobel_prizes/peace/laureates/1964/king-acceptance.html.

9. "Voting Rights Act (1965)," Our Documents, http://www.ourdocuments. gov/doc.php?flash=old&doc=100.

CHAPTER 17—THE DEATHS OF THE DREAMERS

1. Geraldine Watts Bell, "Death in the Morning," *Down Home*, vol. 3, no. 1 (Fall 1982), 18–19.
2. Earl Caldwell, "Martin Luther King Is Slain in Memphis; A White Is Suspected; Johnson Urges Calm," *New York Times*, April 5, 1968, http://www.nytimes.com/learning/general/onthisday/big/0404.html.
3. Martin Luther King Jr., "I've Been to the Mountaintop," American Rhetoric, April 3, 1968, http://www.americanrhetoric.com/speeches/ mlkivebeentothemountaintop.htm.
4. "1968: Martin Luther King Shot Dead," BBC: On This Day, http://news .bbc.co.uk/onthisday/hi/dates/stories/april/4/newsid_2453000/2453987.stm.
5. "James Earl Ray, Convicted King Assassin, Dies," CNN, April 23, 1998, http://www.cnn.com/US/9804/23/ray.obit.
6. Robert F. Kennedy, "The Ripple of Hope," http://bobby-kennedy.com.

CHAPTER 22—THE CALLING

1. "The Universal Declaration of Human Rights," United Nations, http://www.un.org/en/documents/udhr/index.shtml.

CHAPTER 23—THE CHERRY TRIAL

1. Diane McWhorter, *Carry Me Home* (New York: Simon & Schuster, 2001), 259.
2. Yvonne Shinhoster Lamb, "Birmingham Bomber Bobby Frank Cherry Dies in Prison at 74," *Washington Post*, November 19, 2004, B05.
3. Yvonne Shinhoster Lamb, "Birmingham Bomber Bobby Frank Cherry Dies in Prison at 74," *Washington Post*, November 19, 2004, B05, http:// www.washingtonpost.com/wp-dyn/articles/A61428-2004Nov18.html.
4. "BCRI History," Birmingham Civil Rights Institute, http://www.bcri.org/ information/history_of_bcri/history.html.
5. Tiffany Ray, "Sixteenth Street Baptist Celebrates Renovation on Somber Anniversary," *The Birmingham News*, September 15, 2008, http://www .al.com/news/birminghamnews/index.ssf?/base/news/122146652675230 .xml&coll=2.
6. Birmingham Civil Rights Institute, http://www.bcri.org/information/ index.html.

EPILOGUE

1. Martin Gansberg, "Thirty-Eight Who Saw Murder Didn't Call the Police," *New York Times*, March 27, 1964.
2. "The Birmingham Pledge," The Birmingham Pledge Foundation, http://www.birminghampledge.org.
3. Martin Luther King Jr., "Where Do We Go from Here?" August 16, 1967, Atlanta, Georgia, http://mlk-kpp01.stanford.edu/index.php/encyclopedia/documentsentry/where_do_we_go_from_here_delivered_at_the_11th_annual_sclc_convention.

SAMPLE JIM CROW LAWS

1. "What Was Jim Crow?" Ferris State University, Jim Crow Museum of Racist Memorabilia, http://www.ferris.edu/jimcrow/what.htm.
2. "Jim Crow Laws," American RadioWorks, http://americanradioworks.publicradio.org/features/remembering/laws.html.
3. "What Was Jim Crow?" Ferris State University, Jim Crow Museum of Racist Memorabilia, http://www.ferris.edu/jimcrow/what.htm.
4. "Jim Crow Laws," American RadioWorks, http://americanradioworks.publicradio.org/features/remembering/laws.html.
5. Ibid.
6. Ibid.
7. Ibid.
8. "What Was Jim Crow?" Ferris State University, Jim Crow Museum of Racist Memorabilia, http://www.ferris.edu/jimcrow/what.htm.
9. Ibid.
10. "Jim Crow Laws," American RadioWorks, http://americanradioworks.publicradio.org/features/remembering/laws.html.